DEVELOPMENT OF
THE LABOR MOVEMENT

DEVELOPMENT
OF THE
LABOR MOVEMENT
IN
Great Britain, France
& Germany

By

W. A. McCONAGHA

Chapel Hill

THE UNIVERSITY OF NORTH CAROLINA PRESS

1942

COPYRIGHT, 1942, BY
THE UNIVERSITY OF NORTH CAROLINA PRESS

PREFACE

To a world wearied often by the activity of book-writers whose efforts are endless and sometimes seemingly without significant purpose, even so modest a volume as this requires some explanation, perhaps, indeed, some defense.

It is not nor does it pretend to be a work of original research, adding, presumably, to the world's stock of knowledge. It is an attempt merely to put a part of that knowledge into a more convenient form and so to increase its usefulness. Materials familiar to all those who have specialized to some degree in the field of labor relations are often placed beyond the reach of the non-specialist, paradoxically enough, because of their very abundance. The length of the tomes, the minuteness of the topics, the dispersion of sources—these things become effective barriers to all except the most determined.

The cause of this undertaking is a long-standing conviction that a study of labor movements which fails to reach beyond the American scene denies to the student adequate perspective and represents a type of provincialism that increasingly has no defense. The immediate occasion of the undertaking was the disappearance from the market of that excellent little volume by Professor Perlman, *A Theory of the Labor Movement.* By that event students, at least for a time, were deprived of any easy access to a knowledge of labor institutions beyond our national borders. How heavily I have leaned on Professor Perlman's book will be apparent and is gladly acknowledged. Special mention should be made, also, of my indebtedness to Mr. John V. Spielmans, formerly of the University of Wisconsin, for the privilege of reading his unpublished manuscript on *The Development of the*

German Free Trade Unions in their Relation to Social Democracy.

Of those from whom I have received more direct assistance I shall mention only a few. A particular debt of gratitude is due to my colleague Professor M. M. Bober for his careful criticism of the section dealing with Germany; to Jessie Mae McConagha for undertaking the very uninspiring but necessary task of correcting for grammatical form; to Anna M. Tarr for her cheerful and effective coöperation in securing materials not contained in our own library; and finally to the Lawrence College faculty as a group for the creation of an intellectual environment so friendly and yet so vigorous as to compel in the individual some attempt at self-expression beyond that of the classroom and its day-by-day pronouncements.

W. A. M.

Lawrence College
Appleton, Wisconsin
March 30, 1942

CONTENTS

CHAPTER	PAGE
PREFACE	v
INTRODUCTION	1
I. GREAT BRITAIN	8
Structural Aspects of British Trade Unionism	8
British Union Philosophy	14
Formation of a Wage-Earning Class	15
Laissez Faire	17
The Combination Acts	18
Labor and Economic Theory	20
Influence of the French Revolution	24
Freedom to Combine	25
Attitude of Labor	25
The Grand National Consolidated Union and the Chartist Movement	27
Shift in the Point of View of Labor	32
Stable Trade Unionism: The New Model	33
The Amalgamated Society of Engineers	37
The Junta and the Struggle for Legal Status	39
The New Unionism	43
Socialism and the New Unionism	44
The Dockers' Strike and Victory for the New Unionism	48
New Unionism in the U. S. A.	50
Formation of a Labor Party	52
The Independent Labor Party	53
The Taff Vale and Osborne Cases	56
Developments Within the Labor Party	60
Unionism in the War and Post-War Period	64
The General Strike	68
Collapse of the General Strike and the Act of 1927	70
Communism in the Post-War Period	72

II. FRANCE 75
Early Types of Organization 77
French Coöperatives 80
The Commune and the Beginnings of
  Modern Labor Movement 82
Radical Influences 83
Socialist Domination and Confusion 85
The Right to Organize 90
National Federation of Syndicats 92
The C. G. T. and the *Bourse du Travail* 93
Union of the C. G. T. and the
  Federation of Bourses 98
A Revolutionary, Anti-Political Policy Established 101
Revolutionary Syndicalism 105
Syndicalist Methods 113
The First World War and Demoralization 119
Reformism 125
Schism, and the Formation of the C. G. T. U. 129
The C. G. T. U. Returns to the Fold 138

III. GERMANY 139
Labor under National Socialism 139
Beginning of German Industrialism 142
Beginning of the Modern Labor Momevent;
  Coöperation; the Hirsch-Duncker Unions 147
Socialist Influence; Lassalle and the Formation
  of the Universal Workingmen's Association 152
Marx Versus Lassalle 158
Development of Marxism and the Union
  of the Two Factions 161
Bismarck's Attack on the Socialists and the
  Development of the Trade Union Point of View 166
General Trade Union Congress and the Events
  Leading to the Declaration of Union Autonomy 173

Relationship Between Party and Unions after Mannheim; Revisionism	179
The Christian Unions	185
Labor's Mounting Prestige During the War and in the Post-War Period	188
Dualism Once Again	191
INDEX	195

DEVELOPMENT OF
THE LABOR MOVEMENT

INTRODUCTION

WHEREVER there exists an organized, conscious, and continuous attempt on the part of a laboring class to improve its economic status, a labor movement may be said to be in existence. It is obvious that under the terms of such a definition labor disturbances, even labor organizations, are not necessarily synonymous with nor do they presuppose a labor movement. So long as there have been possibilities for human exploitation, gestures of revolt against such exploitation have necessarily followed. These revolts in the past, however, whether ancient or medieval, whether of slaves or peasants or craftsmen, were ordinarily too ephemeral and too highly localized to constitute a genuine labor movement. Such movements are a modern phenomenon, the product of an existing capitalistic civilization.

The basic raw material of such a movement is wage-labor which has developed a consciousness of separate group interest and which, furthermore, has freed itself from such traditional inhibitions of caste or class as would make impossible any revolt against existing institutions or the general *status quo*. Thus labor movements relate naturally to the ideas and institutions of a capitalistic system, with which they tend to be coterminous and against which, either in respect to specific practices or *in toto*, they are in conflict.

Although the ultimate aim of the various unit organizations within a labor movement tends to be identical in that they all envision a better type of environment in which laborers may live, nevertheless the temper and immediate purpose of different organizations have varied as widely as the circumstances which have called them into existence. A hasty survey of the most familiar labor history reveals, for example, such wide disparities as those which distinguish the machine-breaking Luddites, the utopians, the revolutionary anarchists, coöperators, modern socialists, trade unionists, etc.

However, regardless of the multiplicity of the shades of opinion that occur throughout the labor world, it would seem that all differences might be classified, at least roughly, under two alternative headings; namely, conservative and revolutionary.

The conservative ideology is that which sees a fundamental harmony of interest between employers and employees and would foster the existing economic system in order that it in turn might minister more successfully to all of its constituent classes, including labor. Leading proponents of this point of view are the pure and simple trade unionists, whose efforts center around the collective agreement. In the United States this approach has been made familiar by the American Federation of Labor and by the work of Samuel Gompers, one of its early and most effective advocates. In Great Britain it is seen most clearly illustrated in the New Model, which dominated during the third quarter of the last century. It was represented in Germany by the Hirsch-Duncker unions, and in France is largely typical of the point of view of the post-War *Confédération Générale du Travail*.

In this conservative movement the problem of whether the craft or the industrial union is to be favored as the bargaining agency is largely a matter of local conditions and depends on the degree of industrial development and on the type of social background against which organizations must be created. If, as in the early days of the A. F. of L., wage earners are held apart by the mutual antipathies of race, religion, surviving national prejudices, etc., craft unions alone seem practicable. Where, on the other hand, a common social and cultural background exists, where class lines are distinct and a class consciousness awakened, industrial unionism is prevalent and increases in importance as craft lines are obliterated by modern industrial techniques.

In contrast to the conservative point of view and conservative institutions the revolutionary position is based on the conviction that the employing class and the laboring class have nothing in common and that any fundamental improvement in labor's condition must be premised on the destruction or displacement of the entire existing economic system.

Since capitalism as a system is a varied and changing affair, movements aimed at its destruction show a similar tendency to variety. Among these revolutionary doctrines none compares in either academic or practical importance with the Marxian theory of capitalist decline and ultimate labor domination. It alone, therefore, will be briefly examined.

In the broad scheme of things as the Marxian would see it, capitalism performs an indispensable function. It alone is able to generate within itself the raw materials of the coming revolution and of the new socialist society and to direct the march of events unswervingly in that general direction. Until capitalism shall have fulfilled this, its historic function, no force will be able to shake it. Once this function has been fulfilled, however, no force will be able to prevail in its defense. Emphasis among the Marxians, therefore, is less upon the problem of destroying the existing regime and more upon the problem of maintaining an intelligent alertness until in due season it shall have destroyed itself. Premature and ill-timed thrusts against it are to be discouraged as puerile and worse than useless. The workers of the world are called upon to unite, not in order to move to an attack, but in order that they may be in position to take over their new responsibilities when the existing economy collapses due to its own internal stresses.

Key to this conception of capitalist decline is the Marxian theory of value, a bizarre distortion of the discarded cost theory of the classical economists.

The value of any commodity, including labor power itself, according to this theory is determined by the quantity of "socially necessary" labor involved in its creation and so congealed within it. If an employer buys labor at its value and sells labor's product at its value and thereby makes a profit (surplus value), it must be due to the fact that in the productive process labor is able to infuse into the materials for fabrication more units of labor than were involved in the creation of its own labor power used up in the process. If, in other words, the total cost of creating a day's labor is six hours of prior labor, and the day's work in question is extended to twelve hours, a surplus equivalent to six hours of labor appears. This surplus the employer appropriates. Since this is the one and only source of profits—capital yielding no such reward to the user—to the degree that labor is displaced by machinery due to technological changes, the rate of profit, other things being equal, is bound to decline. For profits to be sustained would require an exploitation of labor increasing in intensity to the exact degree that labor itself played a decreasing part in the whole productive process.

Once the basic premise, the labor theory of value, is granted, the path of the Marxian logic is inescapable. The *sine qua non* of a capitalistic system is profits. Yet profits, once achieved, must in the very nature of things be largely plowed back in further investments, converted, that is, into capital goods. This process of capital accumulation by progressively increasing the relative amount of capital employed in industry and so decreasing the relative amount of labor, progressively undermines the possibilities of profit making. The rate of profit, in short, shows an incurable inclination to decline. Corollaries of this are the increasing misery of the workers due to the expansion of the industrial reserve army of unemployed and, because of the persistent overexpansion of productive equipment, the occurrence of crises which increase in scope and intensity until the whole system collapses.

The individual capitalist in his struggle to free himself from the grip of this direful circumstance, by unusual effort or stratagem may elevate himself for a time above the sinking mass but only at the expense of his fellows. The total effect of all the individual writhings is merely to drive the whole mass more rapidly downwards into the economic morass which gradually enfolds it, until finally all disappear, the victims of their several successes.

In respect to programs, the difference between the conservative and the radical position corresponds to the difference in their philosophies.

For conservative movements success consists primarily in securing a greater control of working conditions and of the job opportunity itself. Whether this is done by battling on the political front in the interests of protective labor legislation or on the economic front through the strengthening of bargaining possibilities, the union in some form is indispensable and becomes the goal toward which efforts are primarily directed.

To the radical, on the other hand, bent on replacing the existing system by a different and in his imagination a more benevolent one, unionism, while ordinarily viewed with favor, assumes a position of lesser importance. From the socialist point of view in particular, the union, although convenient as an integrating and educative agency, is not indispensable, and in times past has been featured or discarded according to the fluctuations of circumstance or the whim of dominant intellectuals. Indeed, recognition of the advantages of unionism has not been unmixed with misgivings lest the more immediate and more tangible quality of its achievements might lead to a lessened zeal for the more important, although more distant, revolutionary triumphs. Since revolutionary labor movements seek political domination, for them the weapon of final importance, at least in democratic countries, is the ballot.

Between these two points of view, conservative and revolutionary, there is constant conflict and an ebb and flow in relative importance. To the Marxians there is no possible doubt as to the ultimate outcome. However the situation of a particular country and for a particular moment may seem to deny such an assumption, it is none the less true, as they see it, that the ultimate goal of all labor activity is revolution. With the same inevitability that, as time passes, class lines must sharpen and the class war grow more acute, labor must forsake the illusion of class harmony and accept the idea of the necessity of complete working-class control.

While the birth of the New Unionism in Great Britain and of the Congress of Industrial Organizations in America may seem to support the Marxian thesis, inasmuch as both movements are well to the left of the parent organizations, this drift toward radicalism is much more apparent than real. On the other hand, the evidence of the French and German labor movements would lead to precisely the opposite conclusion.

Against the Marxian assumption of predestination and revolution must be urged the less impressive but more defensible contention that labor ultimately finds its way to a philosophy of opportunism based on considerations of immediate self-interest. During the expansionist phase of capitalism or during cycles of prosperity, when profits are abundant and the problem is merely that of their more equitable distribution, conservatism tends to dominate.

The economic system is obviously successful, and its validity goes unquestioned. In times of recession, on the other hand, or when for specific institutional reasons labor feels itself cut off from economic opportunity or social justice, the pendulum tends to swing in the opposite direction.

Thus the fluctuations of labor's attitude toward the existing social order, it would seem, are not necessarily progressive in any particular direction. These fluctuations represent rather a social barometer marking the rise and fall of labor's confidence in the health of existing economic institutions and the quality of the job and wage opportunities afforded. Granted a reasonable show of success on the part of the existing economy, granted also on the part of the state a reasonable sensitivity to labor's interests, then it seems that it might also be granted that labor's revolutionary inclinations will tend constantly to be overshadowed and neutralized by more practical bread-and-butter impulses.

CHAPTER I

GREAT BRITAIN

STRUCTURAL ASPECTS OF BRITISH TRADE UNIONISM

ENGLAND, the country of the oldest industrial civilization in the world, is likewise the country with the oldest continuous labor movement. The mere fact of this priority is important in that it tends to give to the British movement certain distinctive characteristics.

Subsequent movements, out of the very fact that they were subsequent, found themselves in a world of previous experience in organization and so with some preconceptions of structure and conduct. Subsequent movements also, for the most part, found themselves born into an environment of which the Marxian ideals concerning the trade union and its function were already a part. These movements, consequently, were in a much better position to shape themselves in an orderly fashion, in accordance with some general design, and to proceed steadfastly towards a common and recognized goal.

British unionism, lacking such guiding influences and developing among a people with a greater capacity for compromising, temporizing, and makeshift than for devotion to any abstract principle or hypothetical objective, could hardly be presumed to present an appearance of structural unity and neatness or unvarying consistency of conduct. It did not. Indeed, one of its best-known students has lamented that "viewed from the standpoint of any theoretical system the British trade union movement is merely an appalling chaos of contending atoms."[1]

The structural complexity of this movement is easily observed. In 1920, the year of its greatest expansion,

[1] G. D. H. Cole in the *American Economic Review*, Volume 8, p. 493.

8,334,000 union members were distributed among 1,364 separate unions, many of which were purely local in character and of only temporary existence. Thus, while the total union membership was less than twice that of our own country, the number of separate unions exceeded ours approximately tenfold. The textile industry alone has more than twice as many unions as the entire A. F. of L.

Imagine the feelings of an official of this latter organization, bedeviled always by dualism and jurisdictional difficulties, had he read the following excerpt from the *Locomotive Engineers' Journal* (British) for July, 1926: "The trade union organization here is an incredibly complex matting of powerful craft unions. Do not confuse the Printing Machine Managers' Trade Society with the Machine Menders, or even with the Machine Rulers' Society: distinguish these from the National Society of Operative Printers and Assistants, and this in turn from both the Typographical Association and the London Society of Compositors. These, of course, must not be confused with the Lithographic Printers, still less with Lithographic Artists, or even with the Electrotypers' and Stereotypers' Society. The Association of Correctors of the Press and the Printing and Paperworkers' Society no doubt present no problem to the reader. When he has mastered the exact function of these bodies, and their membership, he may proceed to consider the distinction between The National Union of Journalists and the Institute of Journalists. . . ."[2]

Within all this appearance of disunity and disharmony, however, there is actually a considerable degree of accord. Jurisdictional difficulties over membership and job boundaries occur, it is true, but they are rarely carried to

---

[2] Quoted in Selig Perlman, *A Theory of the Labor Movement* (New York, The Macmillan Company, 1928), pp. 143-144.

the extremes that are witnessed in our own country, for always, in spite of the looseness of its institutional setting, British labor has demonstrated an unusual capacity for mutuality and concerted action. This is due in no small part to a gratuitous advantage which British unions reap from the well-marked class lines that exist in the British social environment. While private advantage has been the dominant motivating influence among laborers there as elsewhere, while the unskilled have suffered at the hands of the skilled, weak unions at the hands of the strong, nevertheless, solidified by social pressures, a definite class consciousness has been created, which on the larger and more crucial issues serves to bind the entire laboring population solidly together. In this respect it might be said that British labor receives as an original heritage a sense of unity and solidarity to which American labor after years of conscious effort has scarcely been able as yet to attain.

Among the institutions which in addition to the unions themselves play a significant part in British trade union affairs three at least deserve attention. They are the federations, the trades councils, and the Trades Union Congress.

The formation of federations has been largely in the nature of a protective adjustment to the increasing size of employers' organizations. Neither in structure nor function are they highly standardized institutions. Membership in a particular federation extends to those unions whose members are engaged in allied occupations or who have some other common interest. Often they end in complete amalgamation of the individual units. Functionally some act as genuine bargaining units, some are merely advisory bodies, some are pooling devices for strike funds, etc. Historically the most important of these organizations has been the General Federation of Trade Unions established in 1899. While formerly it was the main coördinating influence in the trade union movement, that function has been largely absorbed by the Trades Union Congress. Its main function now is to provide strike insurance to its members through the pooling of their strike funds. Other and perhaps more typical examples are Printing and Kindred Trades Federation, Transport Workers' Federation, Miners' Federation, etc.

In contrast to the federations, which are based on kinship of economic activity, the trades councils are purely territorial in nature and include all unionists in a given locality regardless of occupation. In this respect they are identical with the city centrals of the American Federation. Through the trades councils it becomes possible for labor in a given section to achieve a united front on all local issues. This attempt towards local solidarity, which might be called the council's original and elementary function, has been complicated in later years by the fact that, although not directly affiliated with the Trades Union Congress, as territorial units they become a convenient medium through which the Congress may come in contact with the workers, district by district, and so carry on its propaganda activities. Furthermore, since the birth of the Labor Party they have acquired political significance as well. They are in many instances the Party's local manifestation, and with it they are directly affiliated. This has altered their nature somewhat, for to the degree that they have become political bodies they are compelled to extend their membership to include the non-unionists who belong to the Party. This mixed membership naturally has somewhat impaired their purely industrial functions. Broadly, they are to the locality what the Trades Union Congress is to the entire labor movement.

At the head of the British labor movement, occupying the same relative position there that the American Federation of Labor has occupied in our own country, is the British Trades Union Congress.

While alike in position, these two bodies are by no means identical in nature, and no one, surely, should view the Congress as merely an American Federation of Labor in a British environment. The key to the difference in these two institutions lies in the fact that, whereas the Congress exists as the symbol of a labor solidarity which already exists, the A. F. of L., on the other hand, has as its reason for being the creation of at least a semblance of solidarity, which in the absence of the Federation would never occur. American unions, lacking the integrating influence of a deep-seated class consciousness generated within, must accept as its alternative the coördinating effect of some force applied from without. This coercive function in the very nature of things has belonged to the A. F. of L. It follows that the A. F. of L. has been, presumably, the author of general trade union policy, labor's spokesman on all controversial issues, and the final arbiter of all inter-union disputes. If in all of this its conduct, in contrast to that of the British Congress, has at times seemed autocratic and out of keeping with the fraternal nature of a labor organization, the justification is obvious. Unity in the American labor movement comes only in such a fashion and at such a price, and without unity labor's cause is hopeless.

This contrast between the Congress and the Federation was even more apparent in the beginning than at the present time. Formed in 1868, when the problem of legal status was the all-engrossing issue and political considerations consequently paramount, the Congress was originally cast for a decidedly political role. For years concern for the political importance of an appearance of complete labor solidarity led to the exclusion from its agenda of all topics except those on which harmony would be inevitable.

Thus there could be no pretense, even, of solving labor's knotty internal or inter-union problems or of exercising a strong leadership on any controversial issues. The Congress thus denied to itself those precise activities in which the A. F. of L. finds the logical basis for its existence.

Although this was a passing situation and the Congress soon began to play a more normal part in union affairs, nevertheless it gained but slowly in influence and reached the period of the World War without ever being able effectively to coördinate trade union activities or to assume a position of real leadership in British working-class affairs.

In part this weakness was structural. In contrast to the situation common in other countries the British Congress is not an organic entity but merely an annual convention. As such, furthermore, throughout most of its history, at least according to its critics, it has been more of a "holiday parade and a talking shop" than a responsible labor parliament for the careful direction of labor affairs. Formerly the only continuous body of the Congress was the Parliamentary Committee, which, as its name implies, was designed primarily to act as a labor lobby in Parliament. This function, never a significant one, became almost completely empty after the formation of the Labor Party.

The beginning of the upswing from this rather low level of importance came during the First World War. Under the necessity of coming to an understanding with organized labor the government chose to deal with it through the medium of the Trades Union Congress. This put the Congress in a key position for the time and so added greatly to its prestige.

Of more permanent importance than any external changes, however, was the scheme of internal reorganization put into effect in 1921. This change involved the replacement of the outmoded Parliamentary Committee by the existing General Council. This latter body is a continuous organization, and while still lacking any broad and specifically delegated powers in the administration of labor affairs, it certainly goes much farther towards constituting a general staff for the labor movement than the Parliamentary Committee which preceded it. The contrast between the old regime and the new within the Trades Union Congress becomes more apparent when some of the specific obligations of the General Council are brought to mind. Among other things it is charged with the responsibility of coördinating the industrial action of the trade unions, of guarding against unfavorable legislation and initiating legislation that is favorable, of adjusting disputes between affiliated unions, of assisting in the work of organizing, etc.[3]

However, in spite of this extension of the scope and vigor of its action in recent years, the Congress still remains largely as from the beginning a moral influence complacent toward the internal stresses of British trade unionism and exceedingly loath to interfere with the perfect autonomy of its various affiliates. The A. F. of L., in contrast, as already pointed out, is basically a hardboiled disciplinarian before whom the specter of organized labor as a "house divided" seems to warrant any type of intrusion on the otherwise private rights of its members.

British Union Philosophy

To convey some notion of the physical structure of the union movement of a given country ought not to be difficult; to discover for that country some distinctive union

---

[3] After the formation of the Labor Party it became desirable to have some means of generating a policy for and coördinating the activities of both Party and Congress. To meet this need, what is now known as the National Council of Labor was created. Although in this "Cabinet of Labor" the two institutions are equally represented, unquestionably the dominant influence is that of the Trades Union Congress.

philosophy is never easy and in this instance will not be attempted. Laborers everywhere and always are too thoroughly human, with wants too real and too immediate, in environments too lacking in constancy to make it possible for them easily to chart a fixed course in terms of some distant or immutable objective, even granting that such could be found. Since the days of Marx, disputation has been endless as to whether labor, whatever its wanderings from the path of narrow consistency with the socialist doctrines, invariably finds in socialism its ultimate goal; or whether, on the other hand, the more it oscillates between conservatism and radicalism as opposite poles, the more it demonstrates a fundamental sameness of point of view. This sameness consists, it is argued, in labor's evident inclination to choose its weapons always in terms of the exigencies of the time or place, care for results begetting a carelessness for the source of the weapons or the trademarks they happen to carry. Whatever the answer, the spectacle of the British labor movement shuttling back and forth between conflicting ideologies must add something to the interest of the history of its development.

Formation of a Wage-Earning Class

While the modern British labor movement with the trade union as its core is in no sense an offspring or continuation of the craftsmen's guilds which arose in the fifteenth century, nevertheless these two institutions, guild and union, interrelate in a very definite fashion. Within the guild system, during its early history at least, was the assumption of an easy fluidity between its classes, the apprentice evolving naturally and inevitably to the status of journeyman and the journeyman, likewise, to that of master craftsman or employer. Obviously so long as such a system lasted or was able to keep alive a reasonable expectancy among the journeymen that they would inevitably become masters, the probability that journeymen would combine against masters was exceedingly remote. The time for labor organization had not yet arrived.

The eighteenth century saw the gradual transformation of this original circumstance. Masters as a class, finding that they were in danger of having their ranks overcrowded, began to defend the advantage of their position by limiting arbitrarily promotions from the ranks of the journeymen. In this effort they were materially aided by certain economic changes. Industry more and more was finding itself compelled to work with expensive materials and increasingly costly equipment. As financial hurdles of this type became higher, fewer were able to elevate themselves to the position of master, even though otherwise they were perfectly free to do so. Thus journeymen gradually became a permanent wage-earning class, and lines of social and economic cleavage, formerly mostly vertical, revolved to the horizontal axis and remained there.

Nothing in labor history seems more clear than the fact that, whenever any exploited group of workers is cut off from hope of escape either by elevation to the ranks of the exploiters or by finding outlet into alternative activity, class conflicts arise. Nothing, consequently, seems more natural than the fact that, whenever under the guild system journeymen found the obstacles to becoming masters relatively insurmountable and their status a thing of corresponding permanence, they began to develop journeymen's societies. These early organizations with as yet no clear conception of class interest, partly trade unionist, partly friendly societies, and partly purely social institutions, were by direct line of descent the beginnings of the modern labor movement in Great Britain.

This gradual tendency to proletarianization and its accompanying phenomena, a thing long in progress, was brought to sudden completion by the sweeping technical changes of the industrial revolution. By this revolution the class lines of the subsequent industrial conflict were finally and clearly established. On the one hand there was the nascent employing group elbowing its way upwards from its middle-class origin to a position of power and prestige in the new economic system. On the other hand there were the wage earners, sunk now to a permanent proletarian status, bewildered by the change in their economic relationship and unable to understand the nature of the calamity that in the end had so swiftly descended upon them.

Laissez Faire

Concurrent with the economic changes of Britain's industrial revolution and scarcely less important as a factor shaping labor history was the very natural propagation of the idea that the welfare of the nation was at one with the welfare of this newly created and rising class of employing industrialists. As this idea gained in currency, there came the inclination on the part of the state to defer to their interests and to look with an unfriendly eye on all actions or institutions that would impede their development.

During the handicraft period now drawing to a close, within which mercantilistic principles had dominated, there had been the appearance at least of even-handed justice on the part of the state toward employers and employees and their controversies. Laws laid down for the conduct of industry applied equally to both. Now in the confusion of the rapid economic change and under the pressure of the industrialists clamoring for relief from the outmoded regulations of an outworn period, Parliament found itself mentally floundering. Unable to decide what to do, perhaps very wisely it was much inclined to do nothing. Thus, while lip service was still being paid to guild regulations and mercantile principles, in actual practice throughout the eighteenth century there was a steady drift toward government non-interference. It may be said, consequently, that Adam Smith's *Wealth of Nations* (1776), the first great philosophic defense of laissez-faire principles, came to bless with academic respectability what was already a well-established, although somewhat reluctant, practice. Since now, however, thanks to its reasoning, the path of least resistance was made also the path of greatest wisdom, Parliament surrendered itself completely to this unique and happy circumstance. Laissez faire was elevated to the status of a recognized public policy.

This abdication of the state in favor of the free play of economic forces, so far as class interests were concerned, was actually and patently an abdication in favor of the employers. For with the hand of the state removed there was no longer any deterrent to the very natural inclination on the part of the employers to profit to the full by the exploitive power which recent economic developments had placed in their possession. There followed for British labor a time of tribulation such as it had never known before—nor has it known since.

The Combination Acts

As a defense strategy, labor's sole recourse lay in organization. Movements in this direction, however, were stopped almost before they were started by the prohibitive legislation involved in the Combination Acts of 1799 and 1800. These acts, by depriving labor of this, its only available weapon, seemed designed to perpetuate by legislation a condition for which a philosophy of legislative inaction was largely responsible.

The Combination Acts, it will be recognized, involved

nothing new in the history of British jurisprudence. Statutes against combination, supported by the common law concept of conspiracy, can be cited as far back as 1305. The modern application of the idea, however, was quite in contrast to its original conception. Earlier prohibitions were based on the mercantilistic assumption that the determination of conditions of employment was a function solely of the state. Combinations to interfere with this function or to alter the economic *status quo* became, consequently, akin to civil rebellion. Under laissez faire, however, such justification for prohibiting combination was obviously lacking. Combination could be outlawed now only on the plea that it restricted trade, that it was in the nature of a mutiny of servants against their masters, or that it was an unwarranted interference with the rights of the latter to do as they liked with their own.

By these acts practically every form of workers' associations except the purely local sick clubs was to be suppressed. Sir Walter Citrine has conveniently summarized this legislation as follows: "It was made then a crime for two or more workmen to agree together to demand an increase of wages. It was a crime to endeavor to induce, even by peaceful persuasion, any workman to leave his work in order to compel the employer to concede an advance of wages or improved conditions of employment. It was a crime to attend any such meeting or to take a subscription for the furtherance of such purposes. It was a crime to subscribe to any fund which could be used to encourage a workman to leave work or refuse employment with the object of bringing pressure to bear upon the employers."[4]

The extent of the judicial savageries perpetrated under these laws with complete government approval would

[4] W. M. Citrine, *The Trade Union Movement in Great Britain* (Amsterdam, International Federation of Trade Unions, 1926), p. 7.

scarcely be credited were not the evidence indisputable. Through this legislation the degradation of labor was made complete. By the coming of laissez faire it had been cut off at a time of great need from all possibility of deriving help from the state. By the passage of the Combination Acts it was now denied the privilege of organization, the only means by which with any degree of effectiveness it might be able to help itself.

Labor and Economic Theory

If explanation is sought for the apparent callousness of the ruling class in the face of the suffering of the wage earners, it may be discovered, at least in part, in the economics of the time. Seldom has economic theory been able to exert so apparent an influence in fashioning public opinion, for seldom has economics been so susceptible of being fashioned into a weapon of purely class advantage. Devoted to the deductive method, the economists of this period were inclined to hew to the line of their particular bit of reasoning, however that reasoning might counter, or be interpreted as countering, the passing advantage of any particular group. Labor became their chief, if unintended victim. For with their seeming connivance, as we shall attempt to make clear, it became possible to invest the whole dismal labor situation with a halo of ultimate beneficence and to demonstrate with scientific irrefutability that, whatever might be the quality of the misery which labor was then enduring, it was the victim merely of inevitable and uncontrollable forces; that its condition was a thing for which no one was personally responsible and with which no one could successfully cope.

Sharpening the acquisitive instinct of the employers at this time, and so the importance to them of some philosophical defense for their exploitive conduct, was the existing scarcity of capital. As the advantages of machine production became apparent and markets pressed for the cheapened supply of goods, employers found themselves facing a world of unlimited opportunity, to possess which the first necessity was an expansion of their limited equipment. Without that ready access to other people's money which is offered by modern banking systems, capital accumulation had to come largely as a direct result of employers' own savings. The growth of an industry was limited largely by its capacity to plow back its own earnings. This gave unusual stimulus to the pursuit of profits and to the beating down of labor costs to the lowest possible level.

As labor in its extremity, still under the influence of mercantilistic traditions, turned to the state for relief, what could have been more welcome to employers than the discovery by the educated classes with the aid of Adam Smith and his disciples that there was a hitherto unsuspected harmony between the unbridled pursuit of self-interest and the common good, and that any meddling by the state in economic matters was wholly unwarranted? As laissez-faire principles were popularly interpreted, not only did the state lack the power to give to labor any permanent relief; the employer lacked the power to do it permanent injury. Indeed, paradoxically enough, as it was sometimes reasoned, the more selfish the employer the more beneficent the circumstance for labor, for the greater the employer's greed the greater must be his care to preserve and foster every part of the means by which he pursued his own selfish advantage.

If, perchance, the apparent squalor of the factory towns became disquieting or led to any possible suspicion as to the validity of such a comfortable logic, the teachings of Thomas Malthus were always available to pillow completely the public conscience and to guard it against any discomfort which otherwise it might have experienced.

If it were true, as Malthus reasoned, that the race in the grip of a biological impulse moves unerringly to its own destruction as population outstrips means of subsistence, then existing poverty and squalor and all their deadly accompaniments served a most useful purpose. However harsh the method, it is nature's way—the only way in fact—of dealing with the world's most vexing social problem, that of balancing population with food supply. Any attempt at interference with this process is worse than useless, for any lessening of existing misery only invites a fresh inundation of numbers. Thus the humanitarian, however praiseworthy his impulses, does society a distinct disservice, for by easing the painfulness of the symptoms he tends ultimately and inescapably to aggravate the basic difficulty; namely, that of an excess of people.

In the midst of a situation which seemed to preclude generous treatment on the part of employers or any interference in its behalf from an outraged public conscience, labor had no alternative, as was pointed out, except to bolster its existing weakness by organization. Here again, however, economic theory was to join forces with the opposition. For out of the teachings of the classical economists came the familiar wages fund doctrine. This theory by seeming to nullify every argument that unionism was able to offer in its own defense made it appear as a wholly indefensible nuisance.

Do you wish to know the proper level of wages? According to this theory in its baldest form the process is simple. Divide the existing fund of capital available for the payment of wages by the number of laborers receiving wages and in the quotient you will find the answer. It is as simple and as safe from manipulation as the rules of arithmetic. Organization, since it affects neither the dividend nor the divisor in this calculation, cannot possibly affect the quotient. To the degree, then, that the wages of the organized rise, the wages of the unorganized must move equally in the opposite direction. Thus organization merely makes it possible for one labor group to prey on another. Alternative to this, but in the long run no more consoling, is the possibility that a general wage increase may come from an encroachment on profits. Since the rate of profits determines the rate of savings, however, reductions of profits by reducing savings affects directly the future quantity of capital and thus the future wages fund and so the future rate of wages. Thus wage earners of the present profit only at the expense of the wage earners of the future. In general, then, as J. S. Mill expressed it, "more than that [the wages fund] ... the wage receiving class cannot possibly divide among them: that amount and no less they cannot but obtain." The same logic which in this manner demonstrates labor's inability to improve its well-being through its own efforts, by an easy corollary demonstrates with equal clarity the inability of employers to add to its misfortunes.

Few economic theories have been more tenacious than the half-truths of the wages fund doctrine. Few could have been more acceptable to a cruelly acquisitive era. By it alone labor organizations could be condemned, employers absolved from all blame, and legislative interference discredited.

It should be asserted parenthetically, however, that in assessing the role of the economists in the class conflicts of this particular period and in determining the degree of their complicity it must be remembered that what economists teach and what is learned by interested groups from their teachings are often quite different matters. Industrialists and landlords, defending their positions with weapons drawn from the arsenal of contemporary economics, naturally chose them with care and shaped them, perhaps even unconsciously, to serve their own particular purpose.

Influence of the French Revolution

Of much shorter duration than the influence of these economic theories but of greater importance while it lasted was the impression made on dominant classes in Britain by the excesses of the French Revolution.

The same changes which had developed employing and wage earning in Britain into permanent classifications had gone a long way also in developing the country into a land of possessors and dispossessed. As the poverty of the propertyless workers deepened, the owning classes began to acquire toward them an attitude of disdain not unmixed with fear. This latter feeling was swelled to panic proportions as the bloody vengeance exacted by the downtrodden classes across the Channel began to be witnessed. In the excited imagination of the times, workmen became actually or potentially secret revolutionaries waiting only for a favorable opportunity to visit on the British people the terror which the French Revolution had made all too familiar.

Against such a background workers' combinations achieved a new and much more sinister significance. In the public mind they were no longer merely economic phenomena; they were political institutions. Not only did their existence threaten the employers profits; as actual or potential revolutionary conspiracies they were a threat to the existing social order. This in the mind of the government was no time for weakness or sentiment. Industrial centers were filled with spies and provocative agents, and every effort was made to inhibit or stamp out all attempts at organization. By virtue of the inefficiency of the police system, sometimes even with the connivance of employers, some organizations escaped. The government attitude stood always, however, as an impending threat, and, when organizers were so unfortunate as to fall into the hands of the authorities, they were made an example, and unreasonable, often wholly unmerciful, punishments were inflicted.

FREEDOM TO COMBINE

Gradually the savagery with which economists were being interpreted and the savagery also of the application of the laws relating to labor began to lessen. In 1824 the Combination Acts were repealed. For labor this was the first break in a quarter-century or more of legislative oppression which had culminated in the "Six Acts" of 1819. The credit for this achievement goes to the middle-class social reformer Francis Place. But, had better times not intervened to render the position of labor less desperate and less explosive and had the return of order in France not made the horrors of a revolution seem a little more remote, even Place's extraordinary ability for political manipulation would scarcely have turned the trick. As it was, much that was gained in 1824 was lost in the counterattack of the next year. Little save the bare right to organized existence was salvaged.

ATTITUDE OF LABOR

In this victory for labor, labor itself had relatively little part. To the degree that it was aware of the effort in its behalf, it was inclined to observe that effort with sullen, apathetic indifference. Two circumstances may help to explain this seemingly unnatural phenomenon and reveal the mind of the laboring class during this period.

In the first place it is important to remember that the industrial revolution affected British labor in a very uneven fashion. This in turn brought an uneven application of the oppressive legislation which had come largely, either directly or indirectly, as its consequence. Industrialization had brought to textile workers, for instance, complete disaster; but building tradesmen, printers, tailors, etc. were comparatively uninvolved and uninjured. The industrial system in its entirety would doubtless have revealed almost every gradation of dislocation or uprooting. While the Combination Acts had been drawn to apply equally to all kinds of labor, indeed to employers as well, in actual practice employers were never interfered with, and the rigor with which the Acts were applied to labor inclined to vary directly with the degree of labor's degradation. Thus, while the relatively prosperous craftsmen even under the Acts could organize with a considerable sense of security, the downtrodden farm laborers and miners and factory workers, particularly, found the situation quite different. The greater the exploitation of a particular group and the more intolerable its condition, the more it endangered the country's peace and prosperity by its irrepressible desire to revolt. The greater, consequently, must be its surveillance the more summary its treatment and the more exemplary its punishments. Thus those most able to push for legislative reform had least to gain from it, while those who had the most to gain were the most thoroughly cowed and dispirited and ignorant of the possibilities of united effort.

A second consideration operating to the same end and one, doubtless, of much greater importance was the fact that the help which organization promised fell far short of the hope to which the mass of the worst exploited laborers were still desperately clinging. At heart they were not yet a wage-working proletariat; they were largely displaced peasants or journeymen cut off from the hope of becoming independent masters. They were not greatly interested, therefore, in achieving a slightly lesser degree of degradation by the uncertain and limited possibilities of waging here and there a more successful strike or driving a somewhat more successful bargain; what they really wished for was a complete wiping out once and for all of the whole, hated factory system.

Without historical perspective and unaware of the social process, they naturally looked with some disdain on any movement with a limited objective or a suggestion of acquiescence in the rising capitalistic system and clung to the hope that in some miraculous fashion progress might be rolled backwards and restore them to the conditions which obtained before the factory arrived. It is to be expected, then, that when they did organize after the repeal of the Combination Acts, it was on a distinctly revolutionary basis.

The Grand National Consolidated Union and the Chartist Movement

The most primitive expression of the workers' dissatisfaction with the new industrial order was their attack on its most tangible evidence and the immediate source of their trouble—the machine itself. This idea seemed to dominate the so-called Luddite uprising (1811-12) and played an important part in the peasant revolts in the southern countries somewhat later (1819). Such activity, however, was largely sporadic and disorganized and must have appeared even to the ignorant but desperate workers themselves as quite obviously futile.

Such revolutionary sentiment found more significant expression in the Grand National Consolidated Trades Union of Robert Owen and in the Chartist movement, which will now be discussed in that order.

In his attempt to secure the repeal of the Combination Acts, it had been argued by Francis Place, so thoroughly did the general assumptions of the wages fund theory dominate middle-class thinking, that the best antidote to labor's inclination to organize was the privilege of doing so. In no other way would it discover so quickly or so surely the futility of such conduct.

Once the privilege was granted, however, the persistent rush to organize seemed to discredit any such contentions. Climaxing this activity was the creation of that colossus of a day, the Grand National Consolidated (1834).

Laborers had been bitterly disappointed at the outcome of the Reform Bill of 1832. From this bill, for which they had worked hard, they hoped to receive the right of suffrage and with that right the power to compel a more friendly legal environment for themselves as workers. Upon finding themselves excluded from the bill and thus denied possible political relief, with a strong revolutionary sentiment to begin with, they were well conditioned for the bizarre syndicalistic program that Owen was sponsoring.

In the new society as Owen conceived it, the instruments of production were to belong to the users. These users were to be organized into great national companies according to trade. Each company thus organized, except for the general coördinating influence of a Grand Lodge, was to be supreme in its own field. Parliamentary authority and with it all of the traditional political machinery was to be a thing of the past. Workers were to be in complete control.

The appeal of this idea was enormous. Existing unions hastened to link up with the new centralizing organization, and countless new groups were formed. In a few weeks the Grand National had enrolled between half a million and a million members. Never had anything comparable to this rush to organize been experienced. The general strike, interpreted merely as a program of passive resistance, was selected as the weapon by which the old order was to be destroyed and opportunity given for the new to be established.

To this bold threat a counterattack was not long in forming. It was led by employers. Even before the union was fairly established, punitive lockouts began to occur and the "document," equivalent to our "yellow dog" contract, was widely presented. Attempts were made to raise funds to protect those so victimized. These funds, though, were quite insufficient and employers, enforcing their demands by threats of dismissal, were able to secure wide acceptance of the non-union agreements.

The morale of the workers, broken by these reverses at the hands of employers, was then completely shattered by the onslaughts from the Government. No considerations of justice or humanity, it soon became evident, were to interfere with its determination to stamp out this new institution. The weapon chosen for the extermination of the unions was an existing law against the private administration of oaths. To understand the effectiveness of such a means of attack, it must be remembered that British unionism at this stage of its development was everywhere characterized by secrecy and ritualism in which oath-taking played a very important part. A small group of Dorchester farm laborers were the first victims. Accused of no offense except that of administering oaths in their unionizing efforts, they were immediately sentenced to seven years transportation, a penalty which under existing conditions might easily have meant exile for life. This was a shocking barbarity for even a barbarous age, and the whole laboring population recoiled in fright. Following this event the Grand National, too thoroughly disorganized and discordant from the very beginning ever to be welded into a coherent and effective institution, went rapidly and completely to pieces.

To labor, the moral of this debacle, had it been able to understand it, was that any disorganized and disorderly rush on the existing economic system was bound to end in precisely the same fashion. Capitalism, youthful, vigorous, and self-reliant, was now firmly established. Labor, on the other hand, was wholly "immature," too lacking as yet in a sense of solidarity to make possible a unified, well-disciplined attack. Such an attack to be successful must be antedated by years of development and patient organizing effort.

The next important event in the annals of the working class was the Chartist Movement (1838-48).

Basically a reaffirmation of the conviction that salvation to labor must come through the seizure of political power in order to compel a greater governmental sensitivity to working-class interests, it was the logical reaction to the collapse of the Grand National and the demonstrated hopelessness of more direct methods. As a revolt against the concentration of political power into the hands of the upper and middle classes it was a direct sequel, also, to the Reform Act of 1832, which by placing labor beyond the pale of political activity had effectively closed the door to constitutional relief and had confirmed to the government the appearance, if not the reality, of a purely class institution.

While many unionists were to be found among the Chartists, organized labor officially held itself aloof. Few unions had survived the debacle of the Grand National, and these few had little enthusiasm, seemingly, for plunging immediately into a mad struggle for radical political reformism. Quantitatively this abstention had little significance. Chartism soon claimed its two to four million members, while the whole trade union population probably did not exceed 100,000. Credit for this remarkable expansion of Chartism should go not so much to the drawing power of the Chartist formula or of its orators as to the compelling power of the direful economic conditions which labor was bent on escaping. Through a change in the poor laws there was a sharp reduction of relief in 1834, and the institution of the hated workhouses or "New Bastilles." In 1837 there occurred a decline in business, which brought a decline in real wages and a further debasement of the existing low standard of living. Under these conditions labor stood ready to fight in any cause promising relief, almost without regard to the quality of the promises.

The "Six Points" of the Charter, of which the first was merely a demand for manhood suffrage, were of themselves in no sense revolutionary; they were not even new, and with the exception of the demand for annual Parliaments have since been enacted. That Chartism should have been considered a revolutionary movement at all relates to the method used or to be used in gaining its political objectives and, since political success was sought only as a means, the nature of the goal toward which the Chartists would ultimately direct their efforts, once political power came within their possession. This goal—if a movement so discordant and inconsistent may be said to have had a goal—was distinctly radical. The drift of opinion as to the initial methods also was ultimately in the same general direction. As it became more and more apparent how completely insensitive a vote-conscious Parliament may be to the moral suasion of a voteless population, other tactics, it seemed out of necessity, had to be resorted to. And, although the concept of a general strike for a starving body of workers approaches the ludicrous, that idea was persistently toyed with. There were whisperings also of a general armed insurrection, toward which the "Newport uprising" was an abortive and pathetically inadequate attempt.

After ten years of fluctuating and dwindling importance Chartism under the stimulation of the general revolutionary atmosphere of 1848 flared up dramatically only to die out forever in the period of reaction that followed. While it accomplished little for its own day, it definitely foreshadowed events of great importance half a century later.

Shift in the Point of View of Labor

The end of Chartism marks the end of an epoch in British working-class history. With it there passed irrevocably the old idea of complete and sudden social transformation, of the crumbling of one economic system and the creation of another as if at the blast of a trumpet. It marked the end, consequently, of the search for social panaceas and ingenious formulas in terms of which a new heaven and a new earth might be constructed. It marked the end of the time, also, when the thoughts of workers persistently turned backward and the coming of the time when yearnings for the past began to translate themselves into hopes for the future. The reason for this is obvious. A generation had now arisen to which the town and the factory were the normal way of life. Capitalism, successful now and secure through its successes, was in position to lessen its most exploitive tactics. The wage scale, furthermore, near the middle of the century began to turn sharply upwards, and the workers, basking in newfound comfort, began to absorb a middle-class attitude whose essence was a belief in the virtues of free competition and the adequacy of self-help within the framework of the existing economic system.

Those interested in comparisons and analogies will not be compelled to strain greatly to discover in our own country a rough counterpart of this early period in the labor history of Great Britain. American workers, also, during the first three quarters of the last century showed a susceptibility to revolutionary panaceas and wasted much of their energy in a futile groping for some escape from the proletarian status that was fastening itself upon them. Only in the latter part of the century did it seem to strike home that the capitalistic system was unshakable, that, having been born wage earners under its domination, they would probably remain so. From this it followed inescapably that they must turn their attention from the idea of destroying or escaping the existing regime to that of securing the maximum of advantage within it. The ascendance of this conviction was symbolized by the ascendance of the pure and simple trade union philosophy of the early American Federation of Labor. In Great Britain the dominance of the same idea found institutional expression in the coming of the "New Model."

Stable Trade Unionism: The New Model

The years of the domination of the trade union concepts of the New Model, roughly those from 1850 to 1890, are sometimes referred to as the golden age of British trade union history. During the greater part of this interval, unionism was not only expanding; it was solidifying its advances and so making itself a permanent part of the British economic life. Furthermore it acquired at this same time those characteristics which, in the main, the world of labor has in mind when it speaks of British trade unionism.

The basic fact distinguishing this period from that which preceded it, the fact on which all the detail of its history converges, was the acceptance of the existing economic system, the recognition of the validity of its institutions and of their unquestioned capacity for survival. Consistent with this change in general social attitude there came a corresponding change in labor policy. It involved, as already suggested, a complete abandonment of the more heroic and revolutionary ideals of the past and the adoption in their stead of that philosophy of conservative opportunism which in this country we are accustomed to associate with the American Federation of Labor.

So far as field of action was concerned, as between the political and the economic fronts there was a tendency to choose the latter. If a pose of pure "economism" was ever discarded, as it was during the struggle for legal status during the decade of the seventies, it was obviously only to free the unions from the danger of legal extermination, not in order to bring pressure to bear on employers. With the notable exception of the miners and textile workers, labor's general attitude throughout this period was one of anti-étatism, and politics was consistently viewed as a purely defensive weapon.

Leadership under the New Model was no longer to be recruited from the ranks of the magnetic visionaries or self-appointed but often inconstant social reformers, as in the era which had come to an end. Labor's affairs were now placed in the capable hands of a group of hardheaded, practical individuals who as laborers had risen through the ranks to their present positions of trust, a paid labor secretariat. These men in going about to build up a new labor movement on an enduring foundation were as unemotional, as businesslike, and in a sense as materialistic as their capitalistic employers, with whom they now hoped to be able to make better terms.

For its ideology labor now turned to the middle class and absorbed much of the current concepts of laissez faire then sponsored politically by the Liberal Party. To hold to such a philosophy was to depersonalize the labor conflict, shifting attention from the avarice and evil intent of greedy employers and fastening it on the immutable, but likewise irreproachable laws of supply and demand. Here too came a concept of harmony of interest which left little room for industrial warfare. Thus to the argument, drawn from the experience of the preceding half-century, that for labor the strike was a futile and dangerous weapon there could now be added the contention that by sheer logic the strike could be none other than a "barbarous" institution, harming everybody, employees as well as employers and the general public. More nearly in accord with the new point of view was the tendency to warp the demand-supply situation into a little more favorable relationship by making and enforcing apprenticeship rules, by building up immigration funds, by condemnation of overtime, etc.

One should not assume, however, as the unfriendly critics of the period intimate, that the New Model was characterized even in the beginning by an absence of virility and a tendency to buy peace with employers at any price. A glance at the record will show that this was not the case. Nevertheless the point scarcely needs laboring that the position of the unions at this time hardly contributed to a recklessly militant program. Aside from the changes in trade union philosophy already alluded to, it should be worth reiterating in this connection that these unions emphasized to an unusual degree the importance of building up extensive benefit programs. Nothing could be clearer than the fact that funds consumed by industrial warfare could scarcely be made available for carrying on this alternative type of activity and, of course, vice versa. Since these two phases of existing union life were plainly contradictory, as the one was featured, the other, to a degree at least, had to be abandoned.

If labor attitude during this period is to be interpreted in terms of an acquiescence in the capitalistic system, that acquiescence in turn finds a substantial basis for its existence in the tremendous run of prosperity which British industry was then enjoying.

Aided by their priority in the industrial revolution, the British possessed a virtual monopoly of the world's industrial technique. And, as new means of transportation and communication became available, opportunities for the exploitation of that advantage seemed to be almost without limit. Starting with 1850 the next 25 years saw export trade increasing almost threefold. Profits and investments grew greater, and there sprang into existence such a stream of goods flowing back into the country, consumers goods as well as raw materials, that there is little wonder it seemed as if the fountain of economic blessing had at last been opened up, and that unbroken years of plenty lay ahead. Undisturbed as yet by Marxian forebodings concerning hidden diseases actually feeding on this apparent good fortune, laissez-faireism, the ideals of free enterprise and the adequacy of self-help, seemed now thoroughly and finally established.

It is not surprising that labor should have caught the contagion of the times. There was, in fact, a more solid basis for complacence than mere trade statistics and steady employment. Wages, which had suffered a relatively steady decline for almost fifty years, began gradually to rise near the middle of the century, and continued to do so for an extended period. The cotton industry led the way, and before the wave of prosperity ended attained an increase of approximately 40 per cent. Such a circumstance could not fail to have its effect. Increasing well-being is a powerful antidote always to belligerence. Why fight for that which of itself seems to trickle into your hands in quite sufficient abundance?

The Amalgamated Society of Engineers

The union which furnished the "New Model" for unionism, and which, as a pioneer in the businesslike type of union then prevailing, had the flattering experience of seeing its constitution adopted in part or in its entirety by practically every union formed or reorganized during this period, was the Amalgamated Society of Engineers (A. S. E.). This union in a very real sense epitomized the trade unionism of the period and serves as a convenient basis for its further and more objective analysis.

When the Grand National collapsed in 1834, organization did not disappear with it. It survived in an atomized and essentially local form among unions whose interest was almost equally divided between an effort to protect local working conditions and an effort to build for themselves a defense against the terrors of pauperism and the hated workhouses by means of extensive benefit programs. This emphasis on benefits, it is quite apparent, makes the high dues of these unions no mere matter of choice. They were a thing of necessity.

The ramification of the various organizations whose amalgamation resulted in the A. S. E. is baffling and need not be entered into. Suffice it to say that it became apparent at length to the various types of skilled mechanics who made up its scattered autonomous units that local independence was being bought at too high a price. This condition of anarchy in their own relationships made them quite vulnerable to employers' attacks. One employee group was being played against another to their common disadvantage.

The Journeymen Steam-Engine and Machine Makers and Mill Wrights' Friendly Society of Manchester took the lead in trying to weld this mass together. As the result of a combined process of absorption and amalgamation this was finally accomplished, and in January, 1850, the Amalgamated Society of Engineers began its official existence. Its constitution represented a compromise between concentration and diffusion of authority. The administration of benefits was left in the hands of the local societies to be carried on, however, under the strict regulation of general rules laid down by the national union. Thus there was preserved some appearance of that local autonomy so dear to the hearts of British workers. In industrial matters, on the other hand, there was not only the actuality but likewise the appearance of complete centralization. This was created in order to fulfill the real purpose of organization; namely, a uniformity in trade policy and some approach to standard conditions.

In contrast to the more generous, but more impractical ideals of former British unions, which under the leadership of men like Owen and O'Connor strove to bring salvation to all, the engineers proposed to save only skilled mechanics. The principle of exclusiveness, which they thus helped to establish, although appropriate for them and highly satisfactory for the moment, was to become the basis in later years of some of labor's greatest difficulties. In contrast, also, to the cotton operatives and miners, who out of necessity were led to direct their efforts toward protective legislation and who participated successfully in numerous reform acts, the engineers eschewed politics and clung to economic action. As a powerful union of skilled workers capable of protecting their scarcity advantage through the strict enforcement of apprenticeship rules, their position was neither unnatural nor ineffective. It accorded well also with the anti-political bias of the time, an attitude which was based partly on experience and partly on the absorption of middle-class laissez-faire tendencies.

Amalgamation, concern for friendly benefits, centralization under the leadership of paid officials, acceptance of current economics, absence of concern for politics and legislation as an effective working-class instrument, conservatism, exclusiveness—those things which in general earmarked the engineers—these with few significant exceptions earmarked also the trade unionism of the time.

The Junta and the Struggle for Legal Status

Scarcely less conspicuous than the A. S. E. in the affairs of this period was an association built in its exact image, The Amalgamated Society of Carpenters. At its head was Robert Applegarth.

In the world of labor Applegarth of the Carpenters and Allan of the Engineers were the two most prominent men of their time. Around these two, stationed in London, there gathered a small coterie of other outstanding labor leaders, including Guile of the Ironfounders, Coulson of the Bricklayers, and Odger of the Shoemakers. This group, on which the Webbs have fastened the name "the Junta," acting through the London Trades Council, became a sort of unofficial administrative cabinet for the entire labor movement. As such it gave some semblance of that unity and general coherence which was the next logical step in union development, foreshadowing the coming of the Trades Union Congress established later.

Fostering this desire on the part of union leaders for greater labor solidarity was the increasing hostility of employers, a hostility that grew as unionism itself grew, for by the growth of unionism employers were seeing their hitherto unquestioned right to run their own business as they saw fit increasingly threatened.

This employer attitude found expression in the expansion of employers' associations and an increasing resort to the lockout. Irked by these stoppages, public opinion became aroused, and with characteristic inability to allocate fairly the blame for such a situation directed its resentment wholly against labor. Trade unionism, thus, out of the sheer fact of its progress was finding itself in an increasingly hostile environment. Unfortunately, too, in spite of its vigor and apparent strength it was still exceedingly vulnerable. Of this fact it was soon to become aware.

Either of two events that now occurred, each small in itself, might have started the avalanche which would have swept away the whole union structure and left the union movement where it was before its recent revival. One of these events was the blowing up of a non-union worker's house in Sheffield with a can of gunpowder. The other was the refusal of a British court to prosecute a certain union treasurer who had absconded with £24 from the union treasury.

The first incident, the "Sheffield Outrage" (1866), was the spark which kindled the steadily growing antiunion sentiment of the country into a demand for Parliamentary action against the growing trade union menace. A committee of investigation was immediately appointed by Parliament to take up anew the question, dormant since 1825, as to whether legalized trade unionism was in accord with public policy and so deserving of toleration. The second incident, that of the defalcating official, gave rise to the Hornby vs. Close decision (1867), in which the government refused to take action against the delinquent treasurer on the grounds that unions were outside the law and therefore ineligible to receive legal protection. Since under such a ruling union funds became completely exposed, the easy prey of any dishonest union official, the seriousness of this situation, particularly in view of the importance to the existing unions of their benefit activities, was very great.

In each of these cases the issue was identical; namely,

trade union legality. That must now be established beyond question if the achievements of the last several years were not to be completely wiped out.

Skilfully the Junta strove to establish the idea that in spite of sporadic and isolated acts of violence on the part of union members, unions in general and especially the great amalgamated societies, now the center of attack, were thoroughly respectable, law-abiding institutions whose influence was wholly on the side of conservatism. In pressing this point as they did, it may seem that the unions overplayed their hand. At all events, by the Trade Union Act (1871) passed on the basis of their appeal, Parliament did grant to unions their legal right to exist, but only within the limits of these professions of innocence. The law, that is to say, which made union existence legal was immediately followed by the Criminal Law Amendment Act, which tied union hands by making illegal practically every means by which that existence could be made effective.

As a consequence of this stiffened attitude toward labor conduct, largely a more vigorous application of the conspiracy doctrine as it applied to strikes and corollary activity, people everywhere began to be thrown into prison for the most trivial offenses in connection with labor disputes. The thoroughness of this new type of attack is illustrated by the Webbs, who record one instance in which seven women were jailed for merely saying "bah!" to a strikebreaker.

After such a pyrrhic victory as that of 1871 (for obviously unionism could never survive if compelled to a life so circumscribed and so impotent), the Junta and its allies pushed forward more vigorously than ever, looking for real legislative security and relief. The great influx into the union in 1873 and 1874, together with recent extension of the franchise in 1867, were doubtless factors in their success. At all events they emerged with a new law in 1875, the Conspiracy and Protection of Property Act. Since under its provisions no act committed by a combination in furtherance of a trade dispute might be considered a crime unless the same act were a crime when committed in the absence of combination, that is by an individual acting independently, labor seemed to have won for itself thorough-going legal acceptance. It had gained not only the right to organize; it had gained also the right to act in combination. The haunting fear of attack on the basis of criminal conspiracy was at last laid to rest.

This drive for legal status in which threatened defeat was converted into victory, was the crowning effort of 25 years of remarkable, perhaps unprecedented, trade union development. At the beginning of this period unionism had been the victim of almost every conceivable sort of weakness. It was small, discordant, impoverished, and without satisfactory legal status. Its leaders were discredited as "unscrupulous men, leading a half-idle life, fattening on the contributions of their dupes," while its members were viewed as something "between a criminal vagrant and a revolutionist."

In contrast with such a picture is the one in 1875 of a trade union population of considerably more than a million members, well integrated, possessing vast resources, and led by men who compelled the respect of the country. Among employers there was not only an increasing tendency to recognize the unions; there was an increasing inclination also to the attitude that industrial differences were not of necessity an invitation to trial by combat and that many labor disputes might be better settled through the mediation of a disinterested party.

All this having been done, however, the vigor that

had brought existing organizations to this point appeared to vanish, and a spirit of quietism and inertia seemed to settle down over the entire labor movement.

Whether the lethargy that now became apparent is to be explained in terms of an obsession with benefit activities and the careful hoarding of resources, an obsession so complete that all else seemed of secondary importance, whether it was a total surrender to a minority consciousness which recognized that trade unions, after all, lived by sufferance and to be tolerated must show themselves tolerable, or whether it was merely a more complete surrender to laissez-faireism with its implications in favor of class collaboration—all this may remain a subject for doubt and honest difference of opinion. On one point, however, there should be no disagreement; namely, a refusal to go forward was equivalent to a beginning of decline. This was not the end of all possible organized achievement, and, if the unions representing the New Model stopped at this point, in mid-career as it were, others more energetic were bound to seize the banner from their relaxing fingers and carry it forward.

The New Unionism

A dissident and more vigorous minority, in fact, was already beginning to crystallize within the old organizations and as the germ of the New Unionism to move in its turn toward the leadership of the working class.

The keynoter of this group was Tom Mann of the Engineers. As the inclination of the leaders of the older unions to rest on their laurels became more apparent, he became a crusader against their passive attitude. "How long, how long," was his challenging inquiry, "will you be contented with the present half-hearted policy of your unions? I readily grant that good work has been done in the past by the unions, but in heaven's name, what good purpose are they serving now?"[5] John Burns also took up the cause of a more aggressive action and taunted the existing organizations with having "ceased to be unions for maintaining the rights of labor" and having degenerated through their extensive insurance activities "into mere middle and upper class rate-reducing institutions."[6]

When one considers the fact that at this time more than three fourths of the entire working population was not yet included in any organization and because of the prevailing high dues and general exclusiveness had little possibility of joining; when one considers, too, the contemporary social surveys, which showed literally millions of laborers living close to starvation, for which existing unions showed little concern and for which they had absolutely no remedy, the sharpness of the attack upon them does not appear wholly unwarranted.

Socialism and the New Unionism

Unmentioned in the previous inquiry into the arrested development of existing unionism, though certainly a conditioning factor of immediate importance, was the collapse (1876) of that long-time prosperity upon which it had flourished. Geared as it had been to an expanding and successful capitalism, from which it demanded merely a more equitable division of the abundant profits, the New Model had no specific program or plan for years of depression. In a thoroughgoing supply-demand economics what logical place could there be for either industrial or political onslaughts against employers already mired down by the failure of business? Furthermore not only was

[5] Sidney Webb, *History of Trade Unionism* (New York, Longmans, Green, 1926), pp. 383-384.
[6] Webb, *op. cit.*, p. 385.

the depression seeming to nullify the validity of an aggressive bargaining program, but by expanding to excessive proportions the claims for trade union benefits it was consuming the carefully hoarded resources of the unions as well. This situation weakened the faith of existing unions in the ultimate validity of their own program and must have added measurably to a growing tendency toward passivity and hesitation.

The New Unionists, on the other hand, were not impeded by any such moral obstacles. Since they drew their inspiration from socialism rather than laissez-faire economics, for them the result of the recession was precisely the opposite. Here was objective evidence supporting their basic contention that the real and ultimate purpose of trade unionism was not to compel a more equitable distribution of the profits of an inadequate capitalism but rather to work for a new and more effective social order.

While Ben Tillet, Tom Mann, and John Burns, the chief personalities of this new movement, were in the beginning closely identified with the Social Democratic Federation and were thus under strongly Marxian influence, the socialism inoculating the New Unionism was not Marxian. Even had the English mind been more hospitable to abstraction and difficult logic, such could scarcely have been the case. For, however appropriate Marxism may have seemed to the earlier part of the century with capitalism in its most exploitive phase and without the restraining influence of a democratic government, such a philosophy scarcely made sense against the background of 1890. A democratic state in which labor holds a position of power and which by its record of social legislation has demonstrated a live social conscience is scarcely an appropriate place in which to preach class struggle and revolution.

Nor did this revival of socialism represent a return to the Utopianism of Robert Owen, and for a similar reason. The environment that had made Owenism seem realistic was that of an unsympathetic and oligarchic class state in which labor, ignorant, unorganized, and disfranchised, had been practically helpless and without any effective program. The only apparent solution for its difficulty in that environment was the impossible social miracle which Owen proposed to perform. Such conditions now were gone, so, likewise, the seeming appropriateness of such a remedy.

The socialism which began now to stir the working-class mind and to animate the New Unionism was devoid of any direct philosophic antecedents. It was the new theory of social reform by purely constitutional methods evolved by the Fabian Society. Contemporary in its point of view, distinguished furthermore by a practical conservatism, it was particularly appropriate for its British environment. In contrast to other types of radicalism which had existed hitherto in Great Britain, it called for no destructive or extra-legal tactics. Whereas Owenism or Chartism or Marxian socialism could progress only by the destruction of the existing state or by the colonizing of people in communal groups within it, Fabianism called for no such drastic alternatives. On the contrary with slight alterations it accepted the existing political structure and would add to its glory by making it the chief instrument of social reorganization.

Basic in the Fabian concept was a greater and more even flow of goods as well as their more equitable distribution. This was to be brought about through a gradual extension of state control over industry, beginning with those most highly charged with a public interest and advancing as opportunity afforded into other areas. By lessening the importance of private property in production it was hoped that the tyranny of profits would be lessened as well as the prevalence of unearned rewards in the shape of economic rent. Minor assaults on the existing social order were to be made through taxation for reform purposes and by extensive social legislation. In all this it was the intent to proceed gradually and experimentally, combining always "an ounce of theory with a ton of practice."

From even the most superficial examination of the Fabian doctrine one thing becomes unmistakably clear; namely, to the degree that organized labor became indoctrinated with such a point of view, to that same degree would it be compelled to discard the old anti-étatism of the New Model and interest itself actively in political life. If no other vehicle could be found for carrying out its program, a labor party would become indispensable.

The gospel of the New Unionism with its emphasis on collectivism and class solidarity permeated rapidly into the ranks of the unskilled. To these, cut off as they were from any access to existing unions, it seemed to offer some hope of deliverance. It found response also from the younger members of existing New Model unions, who had begun to lose patience with their own lack of progress and with the existing tendency toward the complete abandonment of the unskilled. Thus gradually two opposing ideals came to dominate the labor movement. These, characterized roughly as radical and conservative, in their struggle for supremacy threatened to divide the entire movement into two permanently hostile camps. Happily for labor this dualistic tendency was averted. An incident now occurred of such intrinsic importance as to deliver the entire movement into the hands of the rising and more radical New Unionists. This incident was the Dockers' Strike of 1889.

The Dockers' Strike and Victory for the New Unionism

The unskilled laborers working on the London docks represented the very dregs of the British working population. If they could be successfully organized and through their organization better conditions could be secured on the water front, that would seem conclusively to demonstrate that nothing was impossible so far as a union program for the unskilled was concerned. Incidentally it would seem to demonstrate also that the attitude of skepticism and aloofness taken by the old unions was wholly unjustified and should be abandoned.

John Burns, Tom Mann, and Ben Tillett, the men responsible for organizing and leading this strike, were likewise the outstanding exponents of the New Unionism. Their indomitable energy and enthusiasm, which refused even to recognize conventional obstacles, as compared to the passive, almost fatalistic attitude of the old unionists, was an object lesson in contrasts that was not lost on the British working public. Partly because of recent revelations concerning the appalling conditions of the London poor,[7] public sympathy from the beginning was largely with the striking dockers. And, impossible as it may seem, the strike finally ended with the men in possession of practically everything they had demanded.

The Dockers' Strike with its unusual publicity occurred at a particularly strategic moment. Prosperity was returning, bringing with it a natural tendency to trade union expansion, and, when to this was added the stimulus of the dockers' experience, a revival began to get under way comparable to those of 1833-4 and 1873-4. The

[7] The result of a long and painstaking inquiry into the actual social conditions in London undertaken by Charles Booth had just been published. The poverty and misery thus revealed were startling in quality and extent and profoundly impressed if not shocked the entire kingdom.

greatest activity was among the unskilled, those formerly thought to be unorganizable. Within the year more than 200,000 of these had been brought into the union. The old unions also profited by the general revival and began to find their numbers considerably augmented.

More important, however, than this expansion in total union membership was the shift that was occurring in the union point of view. The new members who joined the old unions as well as the newly created unions among the unskilled supported solidly the ideals of the New Unionism. Symptomatic of the condition prevailing among the old unions and betraying the rather general subversion to the new point of view was the fact that the staid Engineers included among their five delegates to the Trades Union Congress in 1890 Tom Mann and Ben Tillet, leading New Unionists and heroes of the Dockers' Strike. By its conduct of that year the Congress itself demonstrated clearly that it was now under the domination of the new union influence and ideas.

Because the decline of the New Model and the rise of the New Unionism are largely but opposite aspects of the same picture, the deeper and more ultimate causes of the latter's victory have already been largely explained. It remains merely to be pointed out that, while the New Unionism drew its inspiration largely from socialism, it should not be assumed that in this shift towards the New Unionism socialism scored a triumph. Such was not the case. Socialism was not the matter in question. The real issue in British unionism was action versus inaction, and action won.

Of much greater importance than the possible radical implications of this change was the fact that old ideals of individualism, self-help, and exclusiveness now inclined to give way to a greater appreciation of the importance of class solidarity, improvement through social legislation, and as a corollary an all-inclusive system of organization. By this latter change labor was to be put in position to become not merely an industrial force but a political power as well. Furthermore, because the unskilled could never have paid the high dues a huge benefit program necessitated, there was the tendency for unions to lessen the emphasis on insurance and so, "unencumbered" by such activity, to exist as purely fighting institutions.

As a final word concerning this conflict between the old and the new in British unionism it should not be assumed that this was a war of extermination or even a conflict to establish the permanent lordship of one group over or in place of another. The difference which in the beginning placed the two so sharply in contrast, as time passed began to lessen. The older unions, partly wilfuly and in self-defense, partly, too, inevitably and as a result of the natural pervasiveness of the new ideas in all labor circles, found themselves revived and quickened and so adjusted more and more to the newer tempo and point of view. On the other hand the newer unionism could not insulate itself completely against all changes in its own attitude and conduct. As prosperity was succeeded by depression again, many of the poorer laborers who had swarmed into its ranks after the Dockers' Strike fell by the wayside. This had a sobering effect. The program of the New Unionism as time passed became more staid and routinized, and the vigor of action and conviction became somewhat lessened. As old and new were thus gradually bent in the same direction, differences became blurred and gradually ceased to be a thing of significance.

New Unionism in the U. S. A.

That the part played by the New Model in converting the British labor movement from a revolutionary to a conservative basis has been closely duplicated in our own country by the A. F. of L. has already been pointed out. Now that the history of the New Model has been reviewed, it must be apparent that the likeness extends farther than that. Just as the New Model was ultimately confronted by the New Unionism rebelling against its torpor and lack of achievement in a world as yet essentially unorganized, so the A. F. of L. in turn has been confronted by a new unionism, the C. I. O., which hurls substantially similar charges.

However, while the relationship between the new and the old unionism in the two countries is similar, it is not completely identical. The gap separating C. I. O. from A. F. of L. is not so wide, surely, as that which separated the dual movements in Great Britain at the same stage of development. For, while it is true that the A. F. of L. has been scarcely second to the New Model in antipathy to the use of the political instrument and in disinclination to extend itself in the interests of the unskilled and of the working class generally, it is also true that unlike the New Model the A. F. of L. has refused to surrender its weapons or to forsake completely a militant pose. Not only did the New Model fail to fight for the working class as a whole, but by condemning the strike and coercive tactics in general, it seemed to lose the will to fight even for itself. Such a characterization does not apply equally to the A. F. of L. It has never committed the basic error in labor circles of appearing to desert its own. So, whereas both method and scope were issues separating the British unions, for the American unions the attitude to be taken towards the unskilled—that is, the problem of scope—has been the only significant issue.

To the degree, then, that deduction is possible from analogy or historical precedent, it would seem safe to assume that, if the greater differences separating the new from the old in Great Britain could be resolved and bring as a net consequence a mental rejuvenation merely of the entire trade union movement, the lesser differences separating the two American union bodies should eventually terminate in the same desirable fashion. The future, therefore, one might expect, is neither to the A. F. of L. nor to the C. I. O. but to both, each modified so that they become mutual, even indivisible, and capable of working effectively together.

Formation of a Labor Party

The interest of British labor in politics has been demonstrated by its history thus far as a thing of widely varying intensity. The Reform Bill of 1832 and the subsequent Chartist movement both betokened an active faith in the political instrument. In the Chartist agitation particularly no weapon at labor's command, whether strike, petition, demonstration, or actual violence, was left untried in the struggle for increased political power.

Under the domination of the New Model of the fifties, however, this marked political mentality was replaced by one equally distinguished for its degree of indifference to any such type of approach. The willingness of the Trades Union Congress in 1882 and 1883 to defeat proposals in favor of manhood suffrage by heavy majorities indicates an almost unbelievable "low" in political awareness—an attitude made the more remarkable by the strongly political nature of contemporary trade-unionism on the Continent.

While such an attitude was in complete accord with the best interests of the exclusive and self-sufficient unions of well-paid, skilled workers with their effective bargaining power, for that very reason it failed to accord with the interests of the unskilled, who were as yet the bulk of the rising New Unionism. Of necessity their program was almost wholly one of social reform through legislative enactment. For them, consequently, there was no alternative. They were compelled to project themselves into the political arena. It will be remembered, furthermore, that the original inspiration of this group came largely from Marxism with its intense political preoccupation. And, while Marx was soon discarded for the more practical state socialism of the Independent Labor Party and the Fabians, obviously there was nothing in this shift to lessen political interest.

For politically-minded labor the existing situation was far from satisfactory. Its only approach to legislative successes was to canalize its influence on existing members of Parliament through the lobbying efforts of the Trades Union Congress or, alternative to that, to enter Parliament if possible in a Liberal-Labor alliance. The political activities of the Congress were delegated by that body to its Parliamentary Committee. Since membership on this committee was a symbol of attainment in union circles, such membership became the virtual monopoly of the ranking officials of the largest unions and therefore of men who were already quite thoroughly engrossed with the internal problems of their own organizations. These prior responsibilities made any effective discharge of political obligations virtually impossible. So far as a political accord with the Liberals was concerned, while the Liberal Party had indeed contributed some helpful legislation, it was very plain that Liberalism stopped far short of the goal toward which labor's hopes were being directed and that "Lib-Lab-ism" had therefore only limited possibilities.

The Independent Labor Party

Foreshadowing coming political events in the labor world was the fact that in the general election of 1892 three independent labor candidates were returned to Parliament. At the Trades Union Congress of that year those interested in independent political action decided to call a general conference for the purpose of forming a distinct labor party. Among the delegates to this conference were representatives from the Social Democratic Federation, who were British exponents of Marxism, and from the Fabian Society as well as from many local bodies of trade unionists.

Although the avowed aims of the party that was formed at this time were socialistic, for tactical reasons it refused to call itself the Socialist Party and adopted instead the name Independent Labor Party (I. L. P.). In its socialism it veered sharply away from the Social Democratic Federation, whose ponderous Marxian theorizing and revolutionary aims it considered alike unintelligible and unappealing to the average British workman. On the other hand a strong sense of social obligation and ethical imperative with an equally strong sense of economic and political realism seemed to identify it closely with the Fabian Society. Indeed, had it not been for the I. L. P., whose membership was largely recruited from the leadership of the trade unions, the Fabians would have found themselves with no effective way of spreading their gospel and so condemned to pass out of existence without being able to make any definite imprint on working-class thought or conduct. As it was, they had in the I. L. P. disciples who in their crusading enthusiasm became a leavening influence, carrying the new socialist doctrines to every nook and cranny of the trade-union movement and giving to Fabianism a practical importance it could not otherwise have possessed. In strategy only was there any significant difference of opinion between these two organizations, and this difference was but temporary. The Fabians at the outset were content with the idea of "permeating" the existing political parties. For the I. L. P., on the other hand, despair of the success of such a policy was the primary reason for existence. Thus the Fabians stood as the "brain trust" of this new organization and in general accord with its policy.

British labor, however, was not to be stampeded easily into the field of politics. The ideas and prejudices of the last forty years proved tenacious, and the I. L. P., which had hoped not so much that it might be a political power itself as that it might awaken the mass from its political indifference, was finding its record of achievement rather discouraging. The first signal success was a resolution passed by the Trades Union Congress in 1899, which provided for the calling of a special congress of all kinds of labor organizations in order to devise ways of securing a larger representation in Parliament.

The organization which as a result of this resolution was brought into being (1900), designated at first as the Labor Representation Committee, was the organic beginning of the existing Labor Party, a name which was adopted after the successful 1906 election. Membership in the Labor Party was to be by organization, not by individuals, that is to say one became a member by joining an organization which was affiliated or became affiliated with the Party.[8] The original membership included trade unions, coöperatives, and the socialist societies. Among the early leaders were such men as Keir Hardie, Ramsay MacDonald, and Bernard Shaw.

As a concession to the still lingering aversion among trade unionists to the idea of completely independent political action the Labor Party posed at first as a Labor bloc, declaring that its purpose was "to establish a distinct Labor Group in Parliament who shall have their own whips and agree upon their own policy which must embrace a readiness to coöperate with any party which for

[8] In 1918 the Constitution was altered to include individual members.

the time being may be engaged in promoting legislation in the direct interest of labor." Of significance, too, is the fact that a proposal to limit candidacy to members of the working class only was overwhelmingly defeated. Socialist influence was obviously bearing fruit. For, while by its declaration of purpose it was not a socialist institution, the Labor Party thus showed its socialist sympathy and invited the participation of socialist intellectuals. Ramsay MacDonald, socialist and member of the I. L. P., became the Party's first secretary.

In spite of its vigorous propaganda efforts the organization grew slowly. The Social Democratic Federation, unable to secure the acceptance of its Marxian class struggle ideals, seceded. The coöperatives held aloof, and after two years of effort, out of a trade-union population of more than two millions not half a million belonged to any affiliated society.

The Taff Vale and Osborne Cases

Relief from this discouraging progress came from a very unexpected quarter. For some years there had been a gradual attrition by judicial process of the favorable legal status procured for labor by the legislation of the seventies. The climax to this tendency was the famous Taff Vale decision, which after 25 years of fancied immunity left unionism once again exposed to the danger of legal extinction.

The essential facts relating to this incident were as follows. In August 1900 without any authorization from the Amalgamated Society of Railway Servants a strike was called on the Taff Vale railway. Since railway service was considered a thing of public interest akin almost to the army or navy, the strike was vigorously fought by the company, and a large body of strikebreakers was imported. Although it had not approved the strike, the A. S. R. S. now sent its general secretary to take charge, and extended strike benefits to those out of work. In ten days the affair seemed amicably settled. While some acts of violence had occurred during the strike period, it was never alleged that they were committed under union direction.

In spite of this fact, however, the railway company took action not only against the offending individuals but against the Society itself. As a result, and to the general amazement, damages of £23,000 were awarded. Particularly disconcerting was the fact that there was no attempt to prove that the Society itself was responsible for any violence or any criminal conduct. It was charged simply with having injured the company through the mere fact of stoppage and the thwarting of attempts to secure strike-breakers. The whole legal outlook for labor was thus immediately altered.

What might easily happen to organized labor in a world of unfriendly judges with a well-established precedent of this sort to build upon was all too apparent. If, regardless of the conduct of labor, employers were to have recourse to the damage suit whenever they could show that a strike had involved them in losses, then plainly the strike itself had ceased to be an available union weapon. That which had been conceded to labor in 1824 and reaffirmed and strengthened by the legislation of the seventies, unless political pressure could be brought to bear to compel its repudiation by Parliament, was by this decision henceforth to be denied.

It is not strange, therefore, that the "old" unionists who had previously insisted that politics was the way to destruction began now to insist with even greater fervor that through politics alone would they be able to escape being destroyed. The Labor Party was the logical outlet for such a conviction, and during the next year the total affiliated membership was practically doubled.

To labor, the Taff Vale case had been a peculiarly impressive demonstration of the danger of having supposedly friendly legislation distorted and nullified by court decision. Grimly it was determined, therefore, that the new law must be so clear, so inclusive, and so unequivocal that not one crevice should be left for the entering wedge of judicial opinion. To the legal fraternity the legislation demanded and secured (the Act of 1906) was a legislative monstrosity, in that it seemed not merely to restore legal status to organized labor but to single out trade unions for the bestowal of peculiar immunity and legal privilege. Section 4(1) of the Act reads as follows: "*An action against a trade union,* whether of workmen or masters, or against any members or officials thereof on behalf of themselves and all other members of the trade union in respect of any tortious act alleged to have been committed by or on behalf of the trade union, *shall not be entertained by any court.*"[9]

Labor's battle for organized security, for the moment at least, was won, and the Labor Party showed a natural tendency to relax. Events were soon to prove, however, that in the Act of 1906 labor had not won the war; it had merely taken a battle and this was no time for demobilization.

By the events relating to the Taff Vale case and labor's subsequent successful campaign for union security it was made very clear that in the Labor Party labor had developed a fighting arm of no inconsiderable importance. To the opposition, then, unionized labor having been made safe from molestation by the Act of 1906, political labor became naturally next in line for attack.

[9] Italics mine.

This time the chink in Labor's armor was its method of financing its political activity. Since members of the House of Commons still served without pay, the salaries of successful labor candidates as well as their campaign expenses had to be paid from the union treasuries. Had all dues-paying union members adhered likewise to the Labor Party, all perhaps would have been well. Since some, however, were still Liberals or Conservatives in politics or were opposed to labor's political ventures of any kind, it was irksome to them to know that their union dues were going to finance something of which they disapproved. It had always been possible to iron out this difficulty within the unions themselves until a branch secretary of the Amalgamated Society of Railway Servants, Osborne by name, took legal action against his union, seeking to restrain it from using union funds for political purposes. After considerable litigation and appeal the Law Lords decided (1909) that trade unions had no legal right to use their funds to finance any type of political activity.

Without examining the rather tenuous basis for such a finding, attention is called merely to the very obvious fact that to labor's political life the "Osborne Judgment" was a disaster no less complete than the Taff Vale decision had threatened to be to unionization.

Labor's resentment at this new threat was not lessened by the fact that, while based on a narrow interpretation of the letter of the law (1871, 1875) defining the legal status of trade unionism, it seemed in clear defiance of the spirit of that legislation. Furthermore there was more than a suggestion of discrimination in the fact that other voluntary societies, including the joint stock companies, were at perfect liberty to apply funds to political uses without reference to the will of each individual member. Such action was a legal offense only when committed by labor.

In spite of every effort on labor's part relief was slow in coming. The Labor Party was now in the unhappy position of being so small that it could not compel relief but at the same time of such promise of power that political rivals who otherwise might have been friendly were quite content to see it hamstrung in this fashion. It took four years to secure the Act of 1913, which restored labor to practically the same condition that had obtained before the Osborne judgment was rendered. Under this act in order to legalize political contributions it was merely necessary that such conduct be approved by a majority vote of the union, that all such payments be made from a separate "political fund," and that members on request should be exempted from obligation to contribute to this fund without prejudicing in any way their union standing.[10]

By these two Acts, that of 1906 and that of 1913, labor achieved a condition of great independence on both the industrial and political fronts. It now seemed amply safeguarded, and since that time judicial opinion has added to rather than subtracted from the sense of security that it then possessed.

Developments Within the Labor Party

While labor as a political entity was thus struggling to safeguard the position of the whole movement, significant developments were beginning to take place in ideology and conduct.

Although the Labor Party had been created under socialist auspices and reared under the tutelage of socialist intellectuals, in the beginning at least it was far from being a socialist institution. Nor by its original declaration of purpose, already quoted, did it make any such

[10] By the law of 1927 members instead of being allowed to "contract out" must "contract in" in order to contribute to the political fund.

pretension. By the end of the War, however, things were different. The program then announced (1918) called for "common ownership of the means of production" and was unmistakably socialistic in character.

Concurrently there was a tendency toward an increased degree of political unity. The middle-class attitude which had so dominated in the third quarter of the century had found political expression then in a strong inclination not only toward the Liberal tradition but toward alliance with the Liberal Party. In the 1906 election, where for the first time labor asserted itself as a political power, of the 56 labor candidates elected, according to De Montgomery, only 30 belonged to the Labor Party;[11] the rest either as trade unionists or Liberals made up a separate Liberal-Labor group. As the old middle-class convictions were gradually uprooted under the impact of socialist effort, independent candidacies and "Lib-Lab-ism" gradually disappeared, and the labor vote was solidified within the Labor Party.

The outspoken opposition to the War expressed by its leaders and its left-wing element impaired the popularity of the Party and arrested its growth while the War lasted. During the troubled times following the War, however, it expanded rapidly. In the General Election of 1922, despite a decline in trade-union membership, it polled a vote of 4,237,000 and for the first time became the official Opposition. In 1929 with a vote of 8,362,594 it became the leading party and for the second time in six years took over the Government.

It must not be assumed, however, that the vote which put an avowedly socialist government in power was either a socialist vote or a vote for socialism. Neither would seem to represent the truth. The mass of British workers,

[11] B. G. De Montgomery, *British and Continental Labor Policy* (Oxford, H. Muford, 1923), p. 212.

though they may vote the Labor ticket, have never been socialists. The marriage between British socialism and British trade unionism, whose product was the Labor Party, was an affair of pure convenience. The socialists were like a general staff deprived of an army. Strong in creative thinking but weak in numbers, they seemed eternally barred from any practical realization of their program except as it might be achieved through the voting strength of the rank and file of the trade-union movement. The rank and file, on the other hand, was in position to be greatly profited by the integrating, orientating, and energizing influence of the socialist intellectuals. Such a union was bound to be somewhat uneasy and restive unless or until the workers as a whole were led to subscribe more completely to socialist doctrines.

In spite of the fact that for the workers this meant merely the acceptance of the mild permeative and experimental étatism of the Fabians and of the Independent Labor Party, no student of labor needs to be reminded of the difficulty of such an achievement. To British labor, as to labor in general, the labor problem is a thing which is seen not in its perspective but in its detail. It is a thing which is immediate and, being so, cannot be other than a highly atomized and exceedingly concrete affair. Doctrines, therefore, which by nature must confine themselves to the abstract and the general, while they may be seized for the event or appeal for the moment, sooner or later take on the appearance of so much impedimenta. Friction between the socialism and the trade unionism of the Labor Party came to the surface as early as 1907, the morrow of the Party's formation, when a motion to confine Party membership to trade unionists was defeated by a narrow margin. Countering this proposal was a move on the part of the socialist members in favor of an independent socialist party.

In spite of this tendency to right and left wingism within the Labor Party and a lack of complete accord between the Party and the Trades Union Congress, the physiognomy of the political labor movement remained unaltered until 1932. At that time the Independent Labor Party, sponsor, political core, and strongest socialist organization of the Labor Party, ended its affiliation and began again a separate existence as an independent socialist organization.

Back of this secession and the debacle of which it was merely a part is the apparent universal incapacity of radicalism to survive political success in an essentially conservative environment. In 1924 for a short time and again in 1929 the Labor Party had come into office. In each instance there was so much truckling to political expediency, so much concern that a labor government in spite of its reputation to the contrary might appear actually "safe" and conservative, at the same time so little of achievement in terms of distinctive Party principles, that disappointment and internal dissension were inevitable. Although the occasion of the action of the Independent Labor Party was a rebellion against party discipline, had it not been for these irritating demonstrations of conservatism and irresolution, the discontent of the rebels might have been precluded and discipline prevented from becoming an issue.

Preceding this breach but a part of the same picture was the "treason" of the three leaders of the Labor Party, Mr. MacDonald, Mr. Snowden, and Mr. Thomas (1931). Caught in the economic crisis following 1929 and finding themselves not merely floundering but sinking deeper and deeper, these three party leaders as a desperate expedient jettisoned their own organization and escaped to the opposition. There a coalition or "National" government of Liberals and Conservatives was formed on an avowedly conservative basis. From the eminence of their new position they now turned their guns on their erstwhile followers in the Labor Party.

Although this action cleared the air somewhat and relieved the Party of an inharmonious rightist element, politically it brought complete demoralization. It was a blow from which it has not yet recovered.

Unionism in the War and Post-War Period

Later, in the discussions of the French and German labor movements, it will be observed that for them the World War was an unsettling and revolutionary experience. The British labor movement, on the other hand, had reached such a degree of maturity and stability as to be able to take that epochal event practically in stride and in spite of the new environment and new problems so created to remain essentially unaltered.

For British labor the years preceding the War had been years of increasing tension and unrest. Progress toward a better world for laborers to live in had been slowing down to a standstill. With this lack of progress came a widespread feeling of resentment which shaded into an attitude of cynicism and rebellion. For years and in good faith they had devoted themselves to the task of building up a comprehensive trade union structure in the expectation that it would yield tangible bread-and-butter results. Now they were unable to perceive any satisfactory change in their economic status. They had been attracted also by the hope of achievement on the political front and had created a labor party, which, while accepting existing economic institutions and conducting itself in accordance with existing conventions, was designed to advance the interests of their own particular class. Here again, however, there was a feeling of disappointment. Whether their efforts had been economic or political, they seemed equally unavailing. Labor had been running hard merely to escape going backwards.

Inasmuch, then, as conservatism had failed all along the line, there seemed to be nothing left except experimentation with radical alternatives. There was an increasing inclination, therefore, toward more "direct methods" and the adoption of the revolutionary ideals of the French Syndicalists and the American I. W. W.

How far this tendency would have gone must be left for conjecture. It was cut short by the outbreak of the War, which for its duration meant the burying of class feuds, the forgetting of internal bitterness, and the subjugation of all else to the common concern for the nation's military efficiency. The threads that were picked up at the end of the War were not those of the radical interlude which had immediately preceded it but those of labor's more "normal" existence.

The progress of labor politics in the post-War period has already been mentioned. In industry and on the economic front the signing of the Armistice was the signal for a mass of disturbances. A growing opposition to the War had been reflected by a growing number of strikes even before hostilities ended. And now that grievances, often long pent up, need no longer be deferred to the more imperative demands of national safety, this tendency was accentuated. The post-War environment in itself was highly productive of difficulty, for, needless to say, the conversion of a war-time to a peace-time economy is not to be accomplished without an immense amount of friction. The year 1919 was memorable for the number of stoppages. The record shows 1,350 strikes, involving 35,000,000 working days and 2,600,000 workers.

As the more purely war-time difficulties were gradually untangled, it became apparent that the new peace-time norm must differ somewhat from the previous one and that in it there were difficulties that heretofore had not been so troublesome. World industrial technology, for instance, had been moving forward in an accelerated fashion and had brought with it a sharpening of the problem of technological displacement. To add to this difficulty, war-time necessity had brought an increased infiltration of women into the various occupations. Foreign markets, furthermore, were feeling more than ever the effect of the rapid industrialization of other countries, a fact which, if it did not compel an actual diminution in exports, was certainly compelling some changes in kind. A third disturbing fact was the currency situation. While this was a difficulty of wilful creation, it was, nevertheless, of major importance. It arose out of the determination on the part of the Government to return as soon as possible to the gold standard on the pre-War basis. In order to do this a process of deflation was necessary and was immediately begun. However, when in 1925 the gold standard was actually resumed, domestic prices had not yet fallen to the pre-War level. The pound being thus overvalued, exporters faced by this jump in the foreign price of their currency had no alternative except to cut selling prices and therefore to reduce still further their costs of production.

The implications of such a situation in its relationship to labor welfare are very obvious. While the attack on wages would be likely to begin with and center in the exporting industries, it was bound to have much more far-reaching consequences. The coal miners assumed the leading role in labor's defense in the inevitable conflict.

Even before the War began, coal had shown all the signs of a sick industry and labor disturbances were common. At the close of the War this situation was essentially unaltered, except that, inasmuch as the Government's war-time control of the mines was not immediately relinquished, the miners were for a time under direct Government supervision.

In 1919, as the time approached for the return of the mines to their private owners, a strike was threatened not merely for wages and hours but against the return of the mines to private ownership, that is in favor of the nationalization of the industry. Strike action was delayed when a Royal Commission was appointed to investigate the attitude of the miners and to make recommendations. In spite of the fact that the Commission recommended that the mines actually be nationalized, the Government persisted in its refusal. Angered, the miners appealed to the Trades Union Congress to call a general strike. Although they were unable to obtain any support from either the Congress or from the Triple Alliance, which, formed in 1914, included in addition to the miners themselves the railway and transport workers, they struck independently in October, 1920. After a little more than two weeks off the job they returned to work with the promise of some concessions. These concessions, however, were from the Government and therefore due to expire in March, 1921, when the mines should be returned to their private owners. When that date arrived the owners repudiated the previously existing wage scale and asked not only for its reduction but for a return to the practice, which under private management had previously obtained, of making purely local agreements. The miners refused to accede to these demands and were locked out.

By this time it had become quite apparent that the attack on the miners was merely the spearhead of a general thrust against the entire existing wage level and that, if the miners lost, reductions in other industries were bound to follow. Under these conditions the miners were readily joined by their colleagues of the Triple Alliance for a decisive struggle. Since a simultaneous stoppage of the entire Alliance, that is of miners, railroaders, and transport workers, would have paralyzed the country, the situation grew tense. The whole affair began to have less the air of a strike and more that of a revolution. Under these circumstances the Government again decided to take a hand in affairs.

Unhappily for labor's solidarity and thus for the success of the striking workers the conditions announced to a Parliamentary Committee by Frank Hodges, Secretary of the miners, as a possible basis of settlement between miners and operators were immediately repudiated by the miners themselves without consultation with their allies, the railway and transport workers. These latter, irked by the miners' stubborn refusal to come to terms, withdrew their strike notices and forthwith abandoned the strike. The breach thus created not only marked the end of any possibility of bringing the strike itself to a successful issue; it marked the end, also, of the Triple Alliance. In labor circles the day of the announcement by railway and transport workers that they were abandoning the miners has since been known as "Black Friday."

In spite of these reverses the miners continued to stay out until the end of June, when they returned to work thoroughly beaten. In the wake of the miners' strike came numerous other stoppages involving such important organizations as the cotton operatives and the engineers. As might have been anticipated, however, the employers were uniformly successful. Labor was in retreat all along the line.

The General Strike

Succeeding this episode the next important event involving the coal miners and at the same time the most dramatic incident in the post-War history of British labor was the General Strike of 1926.

The determination to return to the gold standard, as has been observed, brought as an inevitable consequence renewed pressure for wage reductions. The miners in an attempt to improve the conditions that had been imposed upon them at the end of their unsuccessful strike in 1921 sought an increase in wages. This demand on the part of the miners was met by a counter-demand on the part of the owners that existing wages be lowered still further. Since once again this dispute between miners and owners seemed to be merely an opening skirmish in a general campaign for wage reduction, the miners were able to prevail upon the General Council of the Trades Union Congress to exercise a power of leadership recently conferred upon it and to undertake the mobilization of all organized labor in the interests of common defense.

The General Council in accordance with this plan thereupon let it be known that, unless in the meantime some basis of settlement agreeable to the miners might be found, a general strike would be called, beginning July 31, 1925. Alarmed by this threat, the Government now entered the controversy and agreed to subsidize the mine owners until May 1, 1926. This was done, ostensibly at least, in order to insure a continuation of the *status quo* until a Royal Commission might once again investigate the mining industry and report on the merits of the existing controversy.

During this period of armistice, curiously enough, there seems to have been no preparation on labor's part for making good its original strike threat if the Royal Commission failed to provide a mutually agreeable basis of settlement between the miners and mine owners. Since the report of the Commission, when it finally appeared, was acceptable to nobody, the General Council was now "on the spot." If it had been bluffing about calling a general strike on the assumption that mere threat would be adequate, that bluff was now called and there was no face-saving way of escaping its commitment. Accordingly May 4, 1926, was appointed as the day on which the strike was to begin.

Although the stoppage which followed is known as the General Strike, it was not a "general strike" in any sense of the term. It did not involve the whole of British organized labor, neither was it motivated by any ulterior political or revolutionary purpose. Beginning with the key industries the strikers were to be called out in successive waves as the strike itself was gradually extended to industries of less and less importance. So far as the quality of the strike was concerned, surely nothing was more thoroughly determined upon by the workers than that it should be exactly as represented; namely, a purely defensive and strictly industrial affair. Notwithstanding this, however, it was immediately stigmatized by the Government as a revolutionary uprising. Troops were called out and a civil-war atmosphere created.

In the tense situation which followed, the restraint of the workers was equalled only by the lack of restraint on the part of the Government. The latter, provocative and uncompromising, seemed bent not only on teaching labor a lesson but on solving a persistently troublesome labor problem by the simple expedient of crushing the laborers into submission. All the while one of the basic difficulties, the currency situation, remained unexamined and unaltered.

Collapse of the General Strike and the Act of 1927

Although the rank and file responded to the strike call with a promptness and solidarity that surprised even its own leaders, the strike itself from the beginning was foredoomed to failure. It had been called hurriedly, reluctantly, without sufficient preparation, without unified leadership, and without a clear conception of its precise or ultimate objectives. Always there seemed to be a dread among the laborers themselves lest the strike, gaining momentum, might get out of hand and become a genuinely revolutionary affair. So always the leaders seemed torn between reluctance to retreat and fear of advancing. Success under such conditions was clearly impossible. The "Samuel Memorandum" was the rock on which the undertaking actually went to pieces.

Sir Herbert Samuel had been chairman of the Commission whose investigation of the mining controversy had just been completed. He, acting wholly unofficially, had collaborated with the General Council in evolving this "Memorandum" as a suggested basis for the settlement of the original controversy between the owners and the miners. This plan, acceptable to the General Council, was rejected by the miners and apparently with very good reason. If the General Council wished to liquidate the strike and needed only some face-saving opportunity, that was now provided by the miners and their obstinate refusal to "coöperate." The General Council was not slow in acting. The general strike order was countermanded and every effort made to get the men back to work.

All those who had gone out in sympathy with the miners, bewildered at this change in policy and resentful of the seeming waste and mismanagement in such an abortive and futile affair, returned gradually to their old jobs under worsened conditions. This left the miners still locked out and as in 1921 with no alternatives except to surrender or to fight alone. They chose the latter alternative and stayed out six months longer or until their resources were completely exhausted. When they finally returned to work, they did so on the mine-owners' terms.

The general strike of 1926 was not only the high-water

mark of labors' post-War industrial offensive; it was one of the most memorable clashes in the whole of trade union history. Its sequel was the Trade Disputes and Trade Unions Act of 1927.

Although this strike had not seriously disturbed the national economy nor had it in any sense threatened established constitutional authority, nevertheless it left the country in a disturbed frame of mind. It had been demonstrated quite clearly that, were a strike to occur with workers less docile and constitutionally minded and at the same time better prepared and more determined—a circumstance not wholly inconceivable—such a strike might have unpleasant and far-reaching consequences. With public sentiment thus favorable to repression, the Government naturally moved to solidify its victory by securing legislation which would safeguard from any recurrence of such an event. The Act of 1927 consequently declared illegal any strike which "has any object other than or in addition to the furtherance of a trade dispute within the trade or industry in which the strikers are engaged" or "is a strike designed or calculated to coerce the Government either directly or by inflicting hardship upon the community."

While this law is obviously open to broad interpretation and its actual severity depends on the position assumed by the courts, as it stands it would seem to outlaw all sympathetic strikes and also to provide in addition that any strike that compels government intervention becomes *ipso facto* an illegal affair.

COMMUNISM IN THE POST-WAR PERIOD

Although the British labor movement had a strong ethical, even religious, inclination, Christian unionism, an institution of considerable significance on the Continent, never gained a foothold in the British Isles. Likewise in spite of a strong socialist trend, there was little inclination to be greatly disturbed by the Russian Revolution or influences emanating from the Communist International. No capitalistic country, however, was wholly immune to the communist influence and the British labor movement was not without its experiences with this type of radicalism. A factor contributing to communist success was the growing conservatism of the Labor Party and the disillusionment which came from its sorry record in office. Operating to the same end was the poor showing made by the trade-union leaders in conducting the general strike. Reaction against these demonstrations of conservatism and ineptitude brought workers of a more radical inclination into the ranks of the communists.

This more radical minority was met by the solid opposition of both the Labor Party and the Trades Union Congress. The Party led the way with a series of defensive measures. In 1924 it refused to permit communists longer to be chosen as candidates to Parliament or even to be accepted as Party members. This was followed in 1926 by the disaffiliation of a number of local organizations for continuing to tolerate communist members. This position was further strengthened in 1930 by a refusal to allow members of the Party to become associated with institutions under communist control. The last gesture against the communists was in 1936, when a motion in favor of accepting the local Communist Party as an affiliate of the Labor Party was defeated by a vote of approximately three to one.

The trade unions in their turn have taken a similar unfriendly attitude. Formerly open to all comers, they voted in 1927 that any trades councils "affiliated to or associated with" institutions under communist domination should no longer be recognized by the General Council of the Trades Union Congress. The attitude of the Congress became the attitude also of many of the larger unions which moved to exclude communists from all offices within the organization. Of the ninety-two unions reporting to the Congress in 1929 on "disruptive elements" only a third, approximately, admitted having had any trouble with communist influences. Yet, in spite of the relative smallness of their number, the communists have continued to exist as a persistently troublesome problem within the general trade-union movement, a movement which, particularly since the destruction of trade-unionism in Germany, has steadily been growing more conservative.

CHAPTER II

FRANCE

SINCE workers' organizations in France are known as syndicats, unionism for the Frenchman becomes syndicalism, and the English-speaking world has been inclined when referring to the French labor movement to use the French terminology rather than its English equivalent.

That labor movements outside of France are often designated as syndicalist movements need cause no confusion. The strong radical inclinations of the French working class during the formative days of French unionism gave to those organizations a peculiar revolutionary tinge which may be characterized roughly as a composite of the ideals of trade unionism, anarchism, and socialism. As this distinctive revolutionary philosophy began to find acceptance in other countries, the name syndicalism in its English usage began to detach itself from its original local connotation and to be applied to any labor movement, regardless of its national environment, which subscribed to this peculiar point of view. Within France itself, since the dominant labor organization, *La Confédération Générale du Travail*, has now ceased to be "syndicalistic" in that it has forsaken the radical creed which marked its beginning, the modern phase of French unionism is known as *syndicalisme réformiste* to distinguish it from the older and more widely recognized *syndicalisme révolutionnaire*.

In comparison with the labor movements of England and Germany, quantitatively, at least, that of France has lacked considerably in significance. In 1906, the year of the appearance of the celebrated Charter of Amiens, there were approximately only 203,000 members within the union organizations. By 1912 there were still not more than about 400,000. Since at this time there was a wage and salaried class in France in excess of 10,000,000, it is obvious that organization was far from complete.

Among the reasons for this seeming under-development, of fundamental importance has been the nature of French industrial structure and the extraordinary size of the French middle class. France has been preëminently the country of the small shopkeeper and of small independent producers of all kinds. In 1911, for instance, it is estimated that there were some 8,500,000 employers in France in comparison with its 10,200,000 employees—a striking contrast to the high degree of concentration which obtains in our own country.

This circumstance has given to France not only a relatively small strictly wage-earning class with a correspondingly large class of hereditary opponents of labor organization; it has meant dispersion of workers in countless small establishments, a no mean obstacle to union activity. It is important in this connection, also, to note that due to the immense ramifications of government economic activity almost one eighth of all French wage earners are employed by the state.

French syndicalism came to the peak of its physical development and its moral influence in the period immediately following the World War, when it included approximately 2,500,000 members. This number, however, due to strikes, internal friction, and depression was rapidly reduced to approximately one fourth of that amount. In 1936 about 950,000 adhered to the C. G. T. These represented the main or syndicalist line of development. In addition there were some 100,000 who belonged to the Christian unions, giving France a trade union population of a little more than a million.

Early Types of Organization

While the formula of the French Revolution was liberty, equality, fraternity, it soon became evident that its dominant concept, that of individualism, was to stand as an unexpected obstacle to labor's subsequent attempts to organize itself. By a law passed in March, 1791, *la liberté du travail* was established, under which the ancient guild system with its monopolistic tendencies was swept away and opportunity thereby created for the rising middle class to enter into any business, trade, or profession whatsoever.

If labor fostered any illusion concerning its status under this law in the new political order, that illusion was soon dispelled. Taking advantage of their legal right to peaceful assemblage, the Paris carpenters organized themselves ostensibly for benevolent purposes but with the underlying motive of increasing their bargaining strength. In response to the cries of protest from the master carpenters the law *Le Chapelier* (June, 1791) was passed. This law, identifying new attempts at labor combination with the recently outlawed guild organizations, represented a complete denial of all attempts at united action. Supported in substance by Napoleon's penal code, which designated as illegal "any coalition on the part of workmen," it remained the official French attitude toward organized labor for almost a hundred years.

It is not to be assumed, of course, that these repressive measures procured for France complete freedom from organization or from labor uprisings during this period. Even during the early part of the century strikes broke out sporadically and sometimes assumed very considerable proportions. These were, in some instances, of political origin; at other times they were almost completely spontaneous; while in still other instances they were created and led by various types of labor organizations which, due to some subterfuge or protective adjustment, had been able to escape the legislation aimed at their general suppression. Outstanding among such organizations were the *compagnonnages*, the *mutualités*, and the *sociétés de résistance*.

The first of these, the *compagnonnages*, whose history extends back to the Middle Ages, were curious organizations steeped in all the mystery of ritual and symbolism and craft jealousies that characterized their early beginning. With their roots well established, and supported by an ancient tradition, they were able successfully to defy both the laws of the Assembly and the Code of Napoleon and came to the peak of their development under the oppressive legislation of the first quarter of the nineteenth century.

Originating among the building tradesmen, the *compagnonnages* continued throughout their existence to draw most heavily from this occupation, although the membership at any particular time might have been considered a fair index of the elite among the craftsmen of that period. The existence of these organizations was very largely due to the itinerant habits of the ancient craftsmen, who journeyed from town to town seeking employment and perfecting themselves in their craft, each hoping to complete his *tour de France* and to become thus a *compagnon du tour de France*.

The *compagnonnages* provided many services for these workers as they moved about and, to a degree, were the forerunners of the later syndical chambers, or union organizations. Members of the same trade lived together, usually at an inn kept by a "father" or "mother," and it was only necessary for an itinerant workman to make himself "recognized" on entering a strange town in order to be received there and to be granted fraternal assistance.

This aid consisted ordinarily of lodging, help in finding employment, care if he were sick, and upon his departure assistance for his journey.

Serving thus as a local bureau of employment and as a clearing house for industrial information, the *compagnonnages* were able to exert a significant economic influence. Labor could be withheld or assisted to withdraw from unfair masters. The flow of labor, furthermore, could be directed, thus making possible the effective labor boycott of whole areas, a condition which could be maintained for long periods, if it seemed desirable.

With the coming of the nineteenth century, however, these ancient institutions began to find themselves outmoded. To the modern world their medieval trappings began to seem ridiculous. Crafts were broken up or disappeared entirely, while industrial standardization and the coming of the railroad made the *tour de France* a meaningless gesture. Attempts at adjustment to the new condition proved ineffective. The *compagnonnages* were too distinctly the product of an ancient regime to harmonize with the needs of a modern industrial society. In the building trades, the last stand of craftism, they were still able to exert considerable influence until the middle of the century. Even here, however, they were failing, and before the century ended had sunk into obscurity or had lost their identity by merging with other organizations.

The second type of organization mentioned, the *mutualité* (mutual aid society) needs no introduction to the labor students of any country. The natural product of the fraternal tendencies of labor in a handicraft period, these societies have served widely as nuclei from which trade unions have developed. Their nominally innocuous function has also gained for them a high degree of immunity from legal interference during periods of restriction. This has made them a common resort under such conditions.

While under the law *Le Chapelier* not even they escaped interdiction, the government made no serious attempt to arrest their development unless it was discovered that they were the outward manifestation merely of a "secret syndicat with compulsory contributions" or were going beyond their strictly benevolent purposes and encouraging strikes and labor unrest. In 1823, there were 123 such institutions in Paris alone, a number which was considerably augmented in the years following.

More distinctly in accord with the industrial conditions of the nineteenth century than either the *compagnonnages* or the *mutualités,* both of which had a distinctly medieval flavor, were the *sociétés de résistance* (fighting unions), which were secretly organized from time to time primarily in the period from 1815 to 1845. Although they were obviously thoroughly illegal, they functioned nevertheless with considerable success, carrying on collective bargaining activities, managing strikes, and arbitrating labor disputes. Their most famous exploit was the direction of the weavers' strikes at Lyons in 1831 and 1834. The most important unit was that of the printers of Paris, organized in 1839. By 1848 it was estimated that half the printers of Paris belonged to this organization. Stimulated by the Revolution of 1848, these societies flourished particularly from that time to the Commune of 1871. After that French workers turned more and more to the syndicat, that is to the openly organized union.

French Coöperatives

In these three types of organization just described there is as yet no hint of that revolutionary quality which was later to distinguish the French labor movement. These institutions were of labor's own creation, spontaneous in their nature and completely lacking in "intellectual" influence or motivation. They were designed to bring about not an overthrow or displacement of the existing economic system but merely a more effective adjustment to it.

However, the seed sown by Saint-Simon, Fourier, Buchez, Proudhon, and Louis Blanc was not destined to lie dormant forever, and after the Revolution of 1848 the idea of coöperation and a vague consciousness of need for complete social transformation began to appear and to dominate the thinking of the working class.

Coöperation, taken up at first with great enthusiasm, resulted in the formation of many societies in the period from 1848 to 1850. In contrast to the successful contemporary English experience the French movement seemed to have been born quite out of season. The societies which survived the first few years of adjustment were dissolved by Napoleon III after his coup in 1851, and France's initial experiment with coöperation was thus forcibly ended. Evidence of the abiding faith of French workmen in the coöperative ideal, however, is the revival of the movement later in the decade of the sixties. Indeed, one of the main functions, presumably, of the syndical chambers which they were then trying to establish and to legalize was the propagation of the coöperative movement. This second attempt, supported by such men as Say, Walras, and Proudhon, while much more successful than the first, was in its turn destined to be dragged down, this time by the failure of the central society, the *Crédit au Travail* of Paris, in 1868. With this second failure, French confidence in coöperation was shattered, and the movement passed without significant achievement or permanent imprint on the character of the future labor movement.

The Commune and the Beginnings of the Modern Labor Movement

At the same time that labor was experimenting so unsuccessfully with coöperation it was making real progress in a different direction and of a much more permanent character. The Revolution of 1848, which had given such an impetus to coöperation, had greatly stimulated, likewise, the creation of such purely proletarian organizations as the *sociétés de résistance*. Increasingly during the years which followed the Revolution the lament of the workers was, "Isolation kills us." The corollary, of course, was a growing appeal for the abolition of the old laws against organization and for the right openly to form syndical chambers, or syndicats, in the various trades. This was considered necessary, it should be noted, not for the purpose of striking more successfully, for strikes were still looked upon with great disfavor. It was the hope, rather, that with the aid of such organizations labor conditions might be improved by mutual and friendly agreements and without resorting to such extreme measures. This apparent moderation, however, should not be allowed to obscure the fact that it was out of the events of 1848 that the French workers gained a much clearer concept of their class interests and a renewed antipathy toward the state, which foreshadowed the later radical and antipolitical qualities of revolutionary syndicalism.

While labor's efforts at this time were not rewarded by an outright repeal of the legislation against combination—this was not achieved until 1884—it did bring a proclamation of *tolérance* (1868) which went far toward achieving the same practical end. With this encouragement a period of rapid expansion in organizing activity set in, a period, however, that was immediately cut short by the Franco-Prussian War and the tragedy of the Commune.

FRANCE 83

By these events, particularly the latter, all previous organizations were completely wiped out.

Radical Influences

Up to this time the French labor movement, composed primarily of the institutions which have just been described, might be interpreted very largely in terms of environment, and represented the spontaneous or at least internally generated attempts on the part of labor to defend itself against the conditions which surrounded it. In the period following the Commune, however, the picture is complicated almost immediately by the activity of the socialist intellectuals, who, gathering a great impetus from the First Socialist International (1864-76), were increasingly vexing the labor movement everywhere with their ready-made formulas and panaceas.

Completely cowed by the ferocious repression of the Commune, labor moved slowly and timidly back into the old channels of its organized efforts. While the old institutions had been swept away, fortunately the achievements of the past had not been wholly lost. The tolerant government policy announced in 1868 was not rescinded, and the desire to organize remained undiminished.

Among the institutions which existed before the Commune and which survived to influence labor's subsequent history, one of importance, certainly, was the International, split now into two bitterly opposing camps of socialists and anarchists. In addition there survived, also, a vigorous remnant of that secret society of revolutionary communists organized by the revolutionist Blanqui during the previous era and known subsequently as the Blanquists. The existence of these well-marked radical groups, Marxian socialists, anarchists, and Blanquists, meant of course that, if and when the time came for a rebirth of organizing efforts on the part of labor, at least three revolutionary forces would be already at hand, each anxious to render assistance and to nudge the nascent movement in its own particular direction.

The initial influence toward a reconstructed unionism actually came, however, from none of these sources. It sprang from an origin that was much more conservative. A republican journalist, Barberet by name, undertook the task, motivated primarily by the desire to do away with strikes, which in his estimation were largely responsible for the downfall of the Second Empire and of whose influence in the new Republic he was quite fearful. The function of the syndicat as he envisaged it was to be largely that of self-help to employees by peaceful methods, the emphasis being upon the mutuality of the interests of employers and employees. The ultimate goal which he had in mind for labor was the creation by the workers themselves of coöperative workshops, through which alone, it was thought, they might gain an equality of economic opportunity.

These syndicats, once they began to reorganize, almost immediately felt the need of uniting into some general organization. Accordingly in August of 1872 *Le Cercle de l'Union Ouvrière* was founded. Created as it was on the morrow of the Commune, needless to say its expression of purpose was couched in language of extreme moderation. Nevertheless the government ordered that it be dissolved.

In lieu of the outlawed *Cercle* the steadily growing syndicalist movement proposed now to attempt, as an alternative device, a series of labor congresses through which something might be achieved toward the same end. The first of these congresses was held in Paris in 1876 and included about 400 delegates from syndicats, coöperatives, and mutual aid societies. This event stands as a landmark in the history of the evolution of the syndicalist movement. While from now on there was still to be much vacillation and much groping, there was thenceforth, none the less, at least some semblance of continuity and individuality in French labor organization.

Socialist Domination and Confusion

Between this first congress at Paris and the third at Marseilles (1879) only three years elapsed, yet within this period that body which at Paris had voted to adhere to the extremely conservative program of Barberet now voted for itself the title of Socialist Labor Congress. In keeping with its title it resolved, furthermore, that it was incapable of doing more than "ameliorating" the condition of a few individuals, that neither producers' nor consumers' coöperation, if it were attained, could emancipate the workers. The aim of the Congress, therefore, was declared to be to procure "the collectivity of soil and subsoil, of instruments of labor, of raw materials— which had been given to all and rendered inalienable by society to whom they must return." Moreover, in order to raise these resolutions above the rank of mere pious gestures, there was organized at the same time the first of that great medley of French socialist parties, the Federation of Socialist Workingmen of France. The Congress of Marseilles, in the mind of Jouhaux, was *"une date capitale"* in the history of French labor.[1] The repercussions from this entrance of labor into politics were "long and difficult to efface." By this act the workers' organization found itself "impeded, fettered, retarded, divided" until its independence of all political affiliations was proclaimed almost a quarter of a century later in the Charter of Amiens.

---

[1] Léon Jouhaux, *Le Syndicalism et la C. G. T.* (Paris, Aux éditions de la Sirène, 1920), pp. 7-8.

In this change of front there is a part which was merely apparent; most of it was real. The Congress at Paris in 1876 was indeed an essentially conservative group, but, in order not to embarrass the new republican government by whose sufferance it existed, it expressed a conservatism somewhat beyond that which it really felt. The reality of the change was largely the product of two coincident developments. In the first place the coöperative movement, around which French laborers had hoped to build up an organization, now seemed incapable of being revived. Thus labor existed for the time being without any program or unifying purpose. It was under these conditions, also, that Jules Guesde, one of the most remarkable of all French socialist leaders, made his appearance. Fresh from a period of exile which had put him in intimate contact with Marx and the International, he was burning with zeal to convert the French laborers into Marxian socialists. In this he was ably, though unwittingly, assisted by the French government, which by its measures of repression and persecution and its obvious unwillingness to interfere in matters affecting the welfare of the workingmen seemed to give point and emphasis to the precise things for which Guesde was contending. The radical tone of the Marseilles Congress was largely a thing of his achievement.

While the French labor movement by this action at Marseilles became officially socialist and committed to the keeping of the socialist intellectuals, it found for itself thereby, as already indicated, not singleness of purpose and unity of mind but quite the opposite. The first breach occurred one year later (1880) at the Congress of Le Havre. The coöperators and moderates (Barberetists), although outvoted, refused to accede to the will of the majority and to join forces with the dominant socialist revolutionaries; consequently they broke away to form a separate organization. In doing this they eliminated themselves as a significant factor in the rising syndicalist movement. After two congresses of their own they disintegrated and faded out of the picture. The main stream of labor influence was to flow, at least for a time, in a much more radical direction.

Although the moderate minority was disposed of by this secession of the Barberetists, unity was not yet achieved. No sooner were the revolutionaries in undisputed control than they began to discover within themselves mutual incompatibilities and irreconcilable differences, which threatened to reduce this majority group to a mass of impotent, warring factions and to destroy all attempts toward labor unity under socialist leadership before such attempts had fairly begun.

First to find the company of the parliamentary socialists intolerable were the communistic anarchists, who, thanks to the influence of Proudhon and Bakunin, were finding French workers unusually receptive to their point of view. Between the anarchist, with his contempt for the state, and the socialist, with his program of political conquest, there was obviously no basis of accord. The anarchists, consequently, following the example of the Barberetists, withdrew to form independent organizations. The socialists themselves, thus "purified," were not able for long, however, to remain in accord. Guesde, a fanatical and doctrinaire Marxian and since 1879 the dominant figure in the French labor movement, evidently hoped to create in France a counterpart of the Social Democratic Party in Germany, with its strong political bent and its close identification with the German trade union movement. "Stolid Marxian materialism," however, with its severe discipline and devotion to orthodoxy, proved very distasteful to the mass of French workers. Consequently at the Congress of St. Etienne in 1882 a majority group under the leadership of Paul Brousse broke away to form the Revolutionary Socialist Labor Party. Those remaining faithful to Guesde adopted the title of French Labor Party (*Parti Ouvrier Français*) and became later in spite of this seeming disaster one of the best organized and most influential socialist groups in France.

The Broussists, representing as they did various types of dissatisfaction with the original Guesdist-controlled organization, lacked the coherence by which the *Parti Ouvrier* was distinguished. While there had been considerable resentment of the autocracy of Guesde and his severe discipline, the basic difficulty, doubtless, was the quality of the Marxian orthodoxy which the Guesdists professed. The contemplation of inexorable, slow-moving economic forces, which rendered equally worthless any attempts at reform or at revolution until assigned historic destinies should be fulfilled, was scarcely in accord with the impulsive qualities of the French mind. The distinguishing characteristic of the Broussists, therefore, was their program of opportunism; whether their method was to be one of violent revolution or one of political permeation, it must be designed to achieve more immediate results. Their strong inclination to a reformist program and to "split up" this program until they made it "finally possible" won for them the derisive nickname of the "possibilists."

The Broussists in their turn now developed a tendency to divide into opposing factions. Dissatisfied with the growing tendency of the majority under its intellectual leadership to devote itself wholly to a program of political permeation or reformism, the more radical minority broke away in 1890 to form still a different party, commonly known as the Allemanists from the name of their leader Allemane. This party was made up largely of unskilled labor and, as its origin would imply, was distinctly revolutionary. As the dominant influence in some of the largest and strongest syndicats it was to become an important factor in shaping the future of the French labor movement.

Although there have been introduced already Anarchists, Blanquists, Guesdists, Broussists, and Allemanists, this is not quite the whole of the story. Another shade of radicalism is yet to be added in the person of the Independent Socialists. Disclaiming allegiance to any particular formal doctrine or to any of the organizations previously mentioned, this group is suggestive of the Fabians of England by its attitude and the brilliance of its leaders, among whom were such notable figures as Jean Jaurès, Millerand, and Viviani. The Independent Socialists were moderates and reformists, striving to unify the dispersed socialist forces behind some program of social reform. By the end of the century they were the most famous as well as the most important unit in the French socialist movement.

In the midst of these various political and revolutionary factions the nascent unions were a "coveted bit" much in danger of being demoralized or pulled to pieces as each group struggled to add to its own power and prestige by obtaining control of these growing organizations. The Broussists, for example, at their congress in 1883 bound each member of the Party to enter his respective syndicat (union group) and to promote the creation of such groups where none yet existed. The Guesdists and Allemanists in turn adopted similar measures.

While such action, to be sure, tended to promote labor organization, the unions when established became the creatures of the particular socialist group which had organized them and in this way were drawn out of the field of normal union activity and into the troubled waters of party politics. They were compelled, furthermore, to make their own the mutual hatreds which separated their sponsors into bitterly competitive groups. As Levine points out, "The adherence of a syndicat to any one socialist group generally repelled the non-socialists and enraged the adherents of other socialist groups, and often led to the formation of rival syndicats in the same trade and locality."[2] Trade unionism was thus in great danger of losing its separate identity and of being swallowed up or sacrificed to the personal ambitions of these rival socialist factions.

The Right to Organize

In contrast to the dispersive influence of this socialist interference and socialist discord strong economic influence at the same time had begun to operate in the opposite direction. French industry had been growing apace, and workers found themselves facing an employer front which was becoming increasingly united. The argument for organization and greater labor solidarity presented by this fact was inescapable. To this influence must be added, also, the encouragement which came from the new law on association, a product of the liberal influence of M. Waldeck-Rousseau and passed in 1884. With the passage of this law the legislation of 1868 was replaced and the period of survival by sufferance, with its virtual compulsion to "approved" reformist methods, at least nominally, was ended. Not only was the right of association fully granted; it became the avowed purpose of the state to stimulate workmen to take advantage of the privileges which under the law they now possessed.

The influence of this legislation as a factor in sweetening the attitude of French labor toward the state and in neutralizing its strong anarchistic tendency is of a mixed quality. While on the one hand there had been bestowed, it is true, the coveted right of association with a gratuitous

[2] Louis Levine, *Syndicalism in France* (New York, Columbia University Press, 1912), p. 60.

gesture of state coöperation, there was withheld, on the other, the right to federate these associations except under narrowly limited conditions. Much more galling, too, than this was the fact that the condition of legality of even local associations was that the name and address of all administrative officers be placed in the hands of the local police. Thus with the same gesture by which syndicats were officially authorized, they were delivered into the hands of the authorities, and their very reason for being was largely nullified—at least so it seemed at the time to the majority of syndicalists. The Congress at Lyons (1886), the first significant event in French labor history subsequent to the law, was called, therefore, not for the purpose of celebrating a new freedom but rather to resent its limitations.

Whatever the real or fancied shortcomings of the law, however, the fact remains that the labor movement, heretofore insignificant in its physical proportions, now entered into a period of steady expansion. In the decade following 1885 the number of syndicats recorded by the Minister of Labor increased from 221 to 2,163, and the anatomy as well as the spirit of the modern French labor movement began rapidly to grow discernible.

The Congress at Lyons foreshadowed these latter developments. As an angry repercussion to the law of 1884, particularly its publicity features, it succumbed easily to the domination of its more radical members. Its spirit was one of opposition to political activity of any kind or to any further entanglements with socialist parties, from whose selfish interests the labor movement had already in their estimation suffered much. The vote by a large majority in favor of the socialization of the instruments of production was evidence of its revolutionary inclinations. Its most significant action, however, was the creation of the National Federation of Syndicats.

National Federation of Syndicats

The first attempt on the part of French labor to federate, the *Cercle de l'Union Ouvrière*, it will be remembered, was born in the unfriendly political environment of 1872 and was forthwith suppressed by the state. The National Federation of Syndicats, although undisturbed by the state, in spite of that fact proved an almost empty achievement, but for more subjective reasons. Unity, unhappily, it was soon discovered, is something more elemental and elusive than gestures in favor of unity. The federating agency, the Federal Council created by the Congress, found itself unable to articulate with the body of individual syndicats. It was thus without effective coördinating or controlling influence. Furthermore the Federation, although conceived as an agency devoted to economic action, fell immediately into the hands of the Guesdists, becoming, it was charged, little more than a tool for the French Labor Party and a training school for Marxian Socialists. Evidence of the truth of these charges lay in the fact that the congresses of the Party were usually held in the same place and just prior to those of the Federation. Delegates to a considerable degree were identical, and the activities of the Federation were largely an echo of those of the Party.

This relationship, and with it the National Federation itself, went to pieces, finally, in the controversy concerning the use of the general strike.

Introduced in the decade of the eighties, the idea of the general strike proved to have a tremendous appeal for French workers, whose emotional temperament seemed so inhospitable to the slow motion of the Marxian formula. Since the strike was a direct denial of Marxism and of the validity of the political program of its French exponents the Guesdists, the latter did their utmost to keep the National Federation and the French labor movement within their grasp and free from such heretical contamination. Their effort, however, was unavailing. At the General Labor Congress (of which the Federation was merely a part) held at Nantes in 1894 the vote stood 67 to 37 in favor of the general strike. The Guesdist majority of the Federation thereupon withdrew from the congress. This was a catastrophe from which the Federation itself proved unable to rally, and shortly afterward it passed out of existence. In its stead and designed to do what it had failed to do, the General Congress at Limoges the following year (1895) laid the foundations of a new organization destined to become one of the most well known of all modern union movements: namely, *La Confédération Générale du Travail*, or, as it is commonly known, the C. G. T.

THE C. G. T. AND THE *Bourse du Travail*

The history of the French labor movement to this time had demonstrated with such unvarying consistency the hazards of political entanglement that it is not surprising that the first article of the *Statutes* of this new organization should declare: "The elements constituting the General Confederation of Labor will remain independent of all political organizations."

This victory for those who would forsake completely the political front in favor of the economic and who would at the same time adopt the revolutionary general strike as the chosen weapon of attack denotes the ascendance of the more radical influences. According to Levine the creation of the General Confederation may well be considered the first important manifestation of the revolutionary tendency of the syndicalist movement of France.

From this radical position, for the present at least, there was to be no recanting or returning. Indeed, as time passed, each succeeding congress expressed with growing emphasis and unanimity that aversion to the political method which had characterized the Congress at Limoges and affirmed, at the same time, an increased devotion to the idea of the general strike. This strike, furthermore, it should be noted, in labor's contemplation ceased to be merely an agency for reform and became rather an emblem of the class struggle—the instrument of social revolution. What, therefore, in its original conception had been easy of acceptance, clothed as it was with the peaceful implications of the "strike of the folded arms," had become of necessity a sterner matter. No strong and growing bourgeois class, labor came to realize, would suffer itself to be expropriated without a struggle. Violence was obviously inevitable along the route which they had chosen to travel. The Confederation in its continued propagation of the idea faced this fact squarely and accepted the issue.

While centralization seems to have been almost an *idée fixe* of the French labor movement and the effort in that direction had been long and persistent, the C. G. T. at the Congress of Paris in 1900, after five years of struggle, was able to report but little more than mere survival. Few new members had joined; others whose membership had been solicited refused or were not even polite enough to make reply. The adhering organizations paid irregularly. The decisions of the Congresses were not executed. Committees did not function because the number of delegates to the National Council was too small; and, had it not been that during these years (until 1902) its congresses invited all syndicats to send delegates, whether they were members or not, these congresses would not even have served as a clearinghouse of ideas nor as a reliable index of the drift of labor opinion.

This situation was due in part, doubtless, to a strong residuum of individualistic or localistic inclination on the part of the French workers, which, economic needs notwithstanding, made them somewhat indifferent, even refractory to schemes for broad integration. A more tangible difficulty, however, and a much more important one was the existence during this period of a vigorous dual organization, distinctive in its nature and peculiarly appropriate to the existing economic conditions and the French point of view; this was the *Bourse du Travail*.

The idea of the bourse or exchange, traceable to the period of the Revolution, was revived near the middle of the century by the economist de Molinari, who had in mind the creation of an employment exchange similar to the stock exchange, where fluctuations in the supply and demand and price of labor should be recorded and made public. For successful functioning, however, any such institution, if of labor's own creation, must await a law permitting not only unions but the association of unions. This law having been passed in 1884, there was established forthwith the *Bourse du Travail* of Paris in 1887 with the coöperation and assistance of the city government. Henceforth the idea spread rapidly, and by 1892 there were 14 bourses in existence. At the outbreak of the World War this number had expanded to 143.

While in the interests of greater freedom of thought and action a few bourses were established in the provinces on the initiative of the local unions and were entirely supported by them, the greater number, following the example of Paris, were established on the initiative of the municipalities and were kept alive by subventions from the public treasury. In spite of this assistance, however, the bourses at their first general congress in 1892 expressed the stoutest determination to allow no "meddling" of government authorities in their functioning. Neither did they permit their growing radical tendencies to be stifled in spite of the fact that the direct financial assistance and the housing facilities of the municipal buildings ordinarily available were thereby either jeopardized or sacrificed.

For students of American labor some progress toward understanding the structure of the bourses may be made by contemplating the trades' unions of our own early history. The competitive area being then essentially local, labor's interest and problems were likewise local and gave rise to that strong tendency toward parochialism in organization which contrasted sharply with the expansive national unions of a later period. The bourse like the trades' union represented organization on a geographic basis, all the syndicats of a given locality, regardless of their craft, joining, presumably, the bourse of that city or region. While this scheme of organization has no exact counterpart in the modern labor movement of other countries, in France it was neither forced nor artificial but a natural response to a lingering handicraftism and to the highly localized areas of competition.

While these bourses were at first essentially labor exchanges and clearinghouses for employment information, their function was expanded with the coming of a more liberal labor policy on the part of the government. To the original employment service and various types of benefit activities, such as sick and unemployment relief, there were now added the services of education, of propaganda, and of resistance. Included under these three headings respectively were such activities as the founding of libraries and the organization of courses of study, the extension of the syndicalist and coöperative movements, and the organization of strikes with provisions, also, for the assistance of those on strike through the payment of strike benefits.

The contribution of the bourses was thus immediate, tangible, and constant and ministered to a very conscious need of the French working class. It was almost inevitable, consequently, that they should have become for the time the most important units in the French labor movement and the key to its development. Almost equally inevitable was the fact that ultimately some attempt would be made to break down their original provincialism and to unite them into some type of national association.

This occurred in 1892. In that year ten out of the existing fourteen bourses joined to form a national organization—the Federation of Labor Exchanges (*La Fédération des Bourses du Travail*).

The impulse to this new organization came not from within, however, but from without and reflected again those socialist rivalries which had been the plague of the French trade union movement. The National Federation of Syndicats, it will be remembered, almost immediately after its organization in 1886 fell under the domination of the Guesdists and became the private weapon of the *Parti Ouvrier Français*. As a countermove now the Allemanists took the initiative in trying to weld the bourses into a federation, with which, it was hoped, they might successfully oppose their old socialist rivals, the Guesdists.

Among the bourses, however, there was little inclination to suffer so effective an economic institution to be dragged back into the troubled waters of empty socialist rivalries and political intrigues. To guard against such an event and to insure, if possible, a continuation of political neutrality, an anarchist, Fernand Pelloutier, was made secretary of the new organization. A man of high ability, Pelloutier is considered the "most able organizer of the working class that modern France has produced." To him must go much of the credit for the material success of the Federation of Bourses as well as that of moulding its political philosophy.

With the expansion of the bourses and the increase in the prestige of the Federation of Bourses the idea was born and gathered momentum that such institutions were capable of reaching beyond the sphere of mere relief and reform and of becoming the basis of a superior social order. This idea was first clearly expressed at their Congress at Tours in 1896.

The very nature of the bourses, it was reasoned, gives them the best insight into the country's economic conditions. Better than anyone else they know the amount of unemployment and the reason for stoppages, the relationship between wages and the cost of living, the amount of goods produced and the amount needed to support the population, etc. Out of this conviction it was not difficult to conjure up the conception of a new society in which the bourses from this vantage point of their intimate contact with the workers' needs and aspirations, as loosely federated associations of producers should assume the direction of the whole social program. The existing political state, in the meanwhile, would be discarded as superfluous or, as the agency of a single economic class, destroyed as actually dangerous. The general social philosophy thus expressed was to become the very essence of revolutionary syndicalism.

Union of the C. G. T. and the Federation of Bourses

When the Federation of Bourses was established in 1892, it will be recalled, there was already in existence, organized in 1886, the National Federation of Syndicats, (succeeded by the C. G. T. in 1895) whose ultimate purpose—the national integration of the labor movement in France—was almost identical with that of the Federation of Bourses. Thus from the birth of the Federation of Bourses and to the end of its separate existence two opposing institutions were pulling at French labor from different directions. Striving for almost identical ends, they advocated different methods of achievement. One advanced the idea of a national association in which the syndicat, that is the trade or industrial union, should be the basic unit; the other advocated an association in which the basic unit should be the local association or bourse composed of all the syndicalist groups in a given locality, regardless of occupation. The former, it will be observed, was based on economic function, the latter essentially on location.

Between these two ideas there is obviously no inherent opposition; they complement as effectively as they contradict. Consequently keen rivalry on both sides was tempered somewhat by the mutual appreciation of the anomaly of any such warfare. In 1902 at the Congress of Montpellier, after some ten years of intermittent chills and fever in their relationship, the two organizations were finally united. The Federation of Bourses, although much the stronger institution, surrendered its name and separate identity—not its existence—and merged with the C. G. T. to create for France one coherent labor body. The total number of syndicats adhering to the C. G. T. at this time was 1,043. The total number of bourses in the Federation was 83—out of the possible 96 in existence. The total membership of the entire organized labor movement was 614,173.[3]

With this unification, dualism in the French labor movement for a time was ended, and French syndicalism achieved that structural form which survives to the pres-

[3] These figures are quoted from Orth: *Socialism and Democracy in Europe*. In general the early statistics of the labor movement in France are incomplete and unreliable. This is due in part to the fact that dues are the badge of union membership and the individual Frenchman hates to pay dues. The membership reports of local unions to the national office were often understated in order to escape this same obligation within the units.

ent time and within which an existing radical tendency was to be matured into that distinctive philosophy known as revolutionary syndicalism.

In this reconstituted C. G. T., workers were now represented both by trade or industry and by locality—by locality through the Federation of Bourses, which now became one of the two principal sections of the Confederation, industrially through the second and other section, that of the Federation of Trades and of Industries and of Isolated Syndicats. The federal union of these two sections constituted that virtual abstraction, the Confederation itself. The General Confederation thus performs much the same function for the Federations of Syndicats and the Federation of Bourses that they in their turn perform for their constituent elements. The worker, in this scheme of things, joins the local syndicat of his trade or industry (after 1906 industrial syndicats and consequently industrial federations alone were eligible to join the General Confederation); it in turn joins the National Federation of Syndicats. As a syndicalist he belongs also to the bourse of his locality, which in turn belongs to the Federation of Bourses. These two superior units join to form the General Confederation, creating that double adherence which distinguishes the organization.

The government of the thus reconstituted C. G. T. was decentralized in nature, guaranteeing the autonomy of each of its constituent parts. Such a scheme of administration was not merely a concession to a general antipathy of French workers to bureaucratic control; it was the expression of a belief in the practical expediency of granting each syndicat freedom to act on its own responsibility. Thus, when the opportune moment came to strike, for example, it might be seized without delaying for the approval of some higher authority and the sacrifice thereby of important strategic advantage. In this connection, however, it is significant to observe that, inasmuch as the syndicats for many years were almost purely fighting organizations, without significant benefit activities or treasury, there was lacking that impulse to strict control which obtains when treasuries are larger: namely, the fear that particular union groups by persistently striking may foolishly or selfishly waste the substance rightfully belonging to the entire body.

Since the physical union of the original C. G. T. and the Federation of Bourses represented the unity merely of divergent conceptions of an appropriate superstructure for the same labor movement, rather than the confluence of two separate movements, it need scarcely be said, that, important as it was to the growth and effectiveness of the organization, it was without particular implication or effect so far as labor's subsequent social philosophy was concerned.

A Revolutionary, Anti-political Policy Established

The strong revolutionary tendency reflected by the previous congresses of both the C. G. T. and the Federation of Bourses bore evidence to the fact that, before the two were united, French organized labor, regardless of its affiliation, was already well within that area designated as revolutionary syndicalism. This particular form of radicalism, holding strongly as it did to the Marxian conception of the class struggle and its corollary the class state, was contemptuous alike of reform by pure and simple trade unionism or of relief by some type of parliamentary action, the program of the socialists.

In spite of its marked extremist tendency, however, as one might naturally assume, the movement as a whole still contained a considerable minority of those sympathetic to one or the other of these milder procedures.

The first trial of strength between reformist and revolutionary elements came at the first congress after the union at Montpellier, the Congress of Bourges in 1904. It was known beforehand that the question of method would be at issue; each side, consequently, made every effort possible to obtain a majority and thus to dominate the policy of the new organization. The reformists, composed chiefly of compositors, tobacco workers, and railway servants, held that violent action on the part of the syndicats was opposed to their own interests; that it would lead to equally violent reprisals on the part of the bourgeois state; and that the encouragement of social reforms, collective agreements, etc., was much more desirable.[4] However, in each instance in which reformism was clearly the issue before this congress, the revolutionaries overwhelmed their opponents by a vote of more than two to one. The C. G. T. thus acknowledged itself to be a distinctly revolutionary body. This fact established, formal decision as to whether syndicalism as a revolutionary movement should seek the overthrow of the existing economic society by violent and direct methods or whether as a political force it should appeal to the more orderly procedure of the ballot box was to become the issue of the next congress, that of Amiens in 1906.

Inasmuch as the latter method, the parliamentary route, represented the program of the socialists, implicit in this decision must come a clarification also of the relationship that was henceforth to exist between these two revolutionary groups; that is, between syndicalists and socialists.

It has already been pointed out that French organized labor began early to appreciate the danger of remaining tributary to the socialist movement, unless, indeed, it had no ambition beyond that of existing as a pawn to the latter's doctrinal warfare or factional strategy. Time and

[4] B. G. De Montgomery, *op. cit.*, p. 47.

again, as syndicalism progressed, it seemed to have laid the ghost of such outside interference only to have it reappear under a new pretext or in a new fashion. The workers of the North in particular had retained a close association with the local branches of the Socialist Party and were eager that a similar relationship be established for the whole Confederation. The socialist case, furthermore, now seemed suddenly strengthened by a structural change within the socialist movement itself.

In the past much of labor's opposition to any socialist alliance had been based, as is well known, on the incoherence of the socialist organization and on its striking tendency to be resolved into a multitude of warring factions. It was felt, and reasonably so, that unity in the labor movement could scarcely be obtained so long as the movement was tied to an organization whose chief characteristic seemed to be its capacity for internal dissention.

The situation was now completely altered. Without reviewing the details of reason or method it will suffice to point out that this divisive tendency in the socialist ranks had been seemingly overcome when, in 1905, the year before the impending Congress at Amiens, French socialists achieved a united front under the title of the *Parti Socialiste Unifié*. In so doing they removed one important argument against uniting with them on a common program.

The case in favor of a socialist alliance, or united action, was presented to the Amiens Congress by Renard of the Guesdist-controlled Federation of Textile Workers. Postulating the advantage of coördinated action on both the economic and political fronts, the resolution which he proposed asked, in essence, that the Congress should declare itself in favor of an effort on the part of the syndicalist movement to secure remedial labor legislation or legislation supporting the class struggle; likewise and to the same end that it should punish by its opposition all persons in positions of power who failed to support such a program. This meant, of course, the virtual commitment of the syndicalist vote to the socialist candidates. Finally it was recommended that the Confederation and the Socialist Party unite on all questions of social reform.

Reformists and revolutionaries alike were united in their opposition to this proposal of Renard's, and it was overwhelmingly defeated. An opposing resolution, framed by M. Griffuelhes, secretary of the Confederation, was carried by a vote of 824 to 3. Inasmuch as this action was not taken in a corner but was anticipated and prepared for by both sides, the vote, it may be assumed, represented considered opinion and not a mere flash of emotion. So interpreted it would imply that syndicalism maintained an almost undivided attitude toward the proposals of Griffuelhes, henceforth known as the Charter of Amiens. As the clearest and most famous official statement of the doctrines of revolutionary syndicalism this resolution is deserving of especial attention.

The particular point at issue was disposed of in the very first paragraph with the declaration that the C. G. T. was independent of all political schools. Later came the clarifying and supporting assertion that, while members in their private lives without the organization were free to hold any political opinion they chose, within the organization they should refrain from introducing the political opinions professed outside of it.

Proceeding then to clarify the general position of the movement, Griffuelhes affirmed that syndicalism adheres to the idea of the class struggle and that its goal is the ultimate emancipation of labor and the destruction of the wage system by means of the general strike. The attention of the movement in the meanwhile is directed to the amelioration of working class conditions through efforts for shorter hours, better wages, etc.

The nucleus of its revolutionary formula was declared to be the syndicat. "Now a group of opposition [it] will be in the future a group of production and distribution, the basis of social organization."

The concluding paragraph of the charter, returning to the issue of the moment, summarizes the syndicalist position as follows: "In so far as organizations are concerned, the Congress decides that, in order that syndicalism may attain its maximum effectiveness, economic action must be exercised directly against the class of employers, and the Confederation must not, as syndical groups, pay any attention to parties and sects which, outside and by their side, may pursue in full liberty the transformation of society."[5]

Since both socialists and syndicalists were concerned with the present welfare of the working class as well as with concepts of revolution, it is evident that, much as they might differ on this latter issue, in spite of themselves they lent mutual assistance in securing a betterment of the conditions of the moment. Not only was this true; the socialists, unwilling to be rebuffed by the vote at Amiens, kept up a constant pressure toward some formal basis of coöperation. The syndicalists, however, were immovable and at the Congress of Le Havre (1912) on the very eve of the World War renewed the pledge they had taken six years before in favor of complete independence of action.

Revolutionary Syndicalism

By the Charter of Amiens the syndicalists went far to dispel the idea that syndicalism was a hopelessly conflicting admixture of socialism and anarchism or that it was merely unionism with a strongly radical bent. Notice was

[5] Léon Jouhaux, *op. cit.*, pp. 147-148.

thus served that, in their own estimation at least, it was neither the one nor the other, rather that a new type of revolutionary movement had come into existence, one whose basic and distinguishing qualities are implied in the oft-repeated formula, "Le syndicalisme se suffit à lui-même," whose spirit is revealed by Paul Louis' sweeping epigrammatic declaration: "Elle [the C. G. T.] est aparlementaire, areligieuse, apatriotique."[6]

Viewed objectively, syndicalism has been defined by Joad as "that form of social theory which regards the Trade Union organizations as at once the foundation of a new society and the instrument whereby it is to be brought into being."[7]

While structurally it presented much the same appearance as the classic British model of union organization, in its philosophy, as has just been pointed out, it was quite at variance. The pure and simple trade unionist, postulating the harmony of interest between capital and labor, is traditionally conservative. The syndicalist, on the contrary, is a thorough-going revolutionist, nothing in his confession of faith being more vigorously adhered to than the doctrine of the class struggle—"the working class and the employing class have nothing in common." Towards labor's present, unionist and syndicalist have in common a mutual interest; toward its future they are poles apart. For, while unionism has no "ultimate purpose," in the syndicalist movement the ultimate purpose represents the very mainspring of its present existence.

Between syndicalism and anarchism there is an obvious similarity, so much in fact that contemporary critics insisted that every objection that could be raised against anarchism applied to syndicalism also. The thumb-prints of anarchist influence are, it is true, quite visible within

[6] Paul Louis, *Le Syndicalisme Français* (Paris, F. Alcan, 1924), p. 12.
[7] C. E. M. Joad, *Modern Political Theory* (Oxford, The Clarendon Press, 1923), p. 63.

the syndicalist formula. Syndicalist and anarchist are at one in deploring the existence of the state and in opposing its various manifestations. Both, furthermore, foster the hope of its ultimate overthrow by direct and violent methods. Here, however, likeness tends to vanish. Anarchism is a species of individualism, a "natural society" where the individual is supreme and his action spontaneous, and its appeal is addressed to everyone without discrimination. Syndicalism, in contrast, extols the virtues of a type of producers' coöperation and is designed for the benefit of the proletariat alone. Closely related is the additional fact that the cell of the future anarchist society is the individual as such, while the cell of the syndicalist society is to be the labor organization, individuals signifying here only as members of such institutions.

So far, however, as syndicalism's kinship to contemporary movements was concerned, both practically and theoretically the closest relationship was to socialism. Syndicalism and socialism in French economic society were both going concerns, each engaged in the difficult business of bettering the immediate as well as the ultimate condition of the French working class. When, therefore, in terms primarily of an effective program for the present, Renard at Amiens had urged collaboration between the two, no one could deny the force in his contention. Furthermore, and aside from considerations of expediency, to a considerable degree both spoke the same language. Both addressed themselves exclusively to the industrial proletariat and rallied equally to the Marxian exhortation "working men of all countries, unite." The idea of the class struggle, moreover, the key to the Marxian formula, was nowhere more jealously adhered to than in the ranks of the syndicalists. Toward the existing bourgeois state, syndicalists and socialists united, also, in their declaration of open warfare, and both abjured in this connection the tendency toward nationalism and militarism with its complement of large standing armies. "Syndicalism," said Paul Louis, "rejects the idea of a fatherland, for the laborer belongs to his class not to his country and the actual frontiers are those of the class and not those of the state; syndicalism combats militarism and proclaims the suppression of the army which enlists the masses of workers and peasants for the service of a directing oligarchy . . . for the function of defending the owner against the worker."[8] To the Marxian this certainly has no unfamiliar ring.

Why, then, it must invariably be asked, did the syndicalists so bluntly refuse at Amiens to make common cause with the socialists for the achievement of an essentially common purpose? The readiest answer seems to lie in the fact that within this appearance of likeness was at least one irreconcilable doctrinal difference which, if adhered to, must hold the two groups forever apart. This difference lies in their conflicting attitude toward the state. While they agree in their attitude toward the existing "bourgeois" state, a difficulty immediately presents itself once the destruction of this state is accomplished. The enmity of the syndicalists directs itself not merely against bourgeois control but against any control whatsoever. The socialists, on the other hand, would destroy the existing state only for the express purpose of replacing it with another—the dictatorship of the proletariat—in which the syndicalists have no assurance that conditions will be more to their liking, or power less oppressive than at present.

However, to assert a willingness on the part of French workers to sacrifice an effective program on the altar of doctrinal consistency alone, would be to claim for them a unique distinction. A priori it would seem that other fac-

[8] Paul Louis, *op. cit.*, p. 15.

tors must have influenced their course of action and, in the balancing of attitudes pro and con, have become the final decisive influence shifting the scale of syndicalist opinion so decidedly against the state and, consequently, against any alliance with the politically minded Socialist Party. Some of these are worthy of mention.

In the first place it will not be forgotten that for the French worker Marxism was an importation. The indigenous radical philosophy of nineteenth-century France was that of Proudhon, "father of modern anarchism," whose anti-authoritarian tendencies created an admirable background for the later efforts of the anarchist Bakunin. Temperamentally responsive to the individualism of the anarchist doctrine, a considerable body of French workers became converted to this general point of view. This group, at first contemptuous of syndicalism, regarding it as a compromising and temporizing affair, grew weary, ultimately, of the futility of their own independent effort and began in the decade of the nineties to join the syndicats. Here they exerted a considerable influence, emphasizing an existing tendency to an anti-socialist, anti-parliamentarian attitude, a point of view which was clearly expressed in the current contention, "all politicians are betrayers."

Sharpening the attitude of these anarchists within the syndicalist movement was the fact that the original heroic quality of Marxism was everywhere beginning to weaken. Socialists more and more were assuming the role and adopting the methods of an ordinary political party, with the customary angling for members and political bargaining and trading. Under these conditions class lines were inevitably weakening and revolutionary purpose submerged or forgotten. To the more radical, then, out of these circumstances syndicalism became a last hope, a final place of refuge. It alone kept pure its original class character, and in it alone the sacred fires of the revolution were still vigorously burning. Jealously now, and at all costs, they felt they must seek to defend it against any affiliations or commitments that would jeopardize to the slightest degree its original revolutionary quality or dim its original revolutionary purpose.

Differing slightly in its nature but identical in its consequence was a working-class resentment against the established order—a resentment which found its beginnings in the disappointments arising out of the Great Revolution itself. Having striven there for deliverance from the oppression of the old regime, the workers eventually found that they had not improved their status by one iota; they had changed the character of the oppressor but they had not escaped oppression. The social legislation following the Revolution had been framed, they felt, not for them but for their control. What they had hoped for themselves, the rising industrial bourgeoisie had appropriated. It was into the hands of the bourgeoisie that the political domination of the nation had fallen, and it was against this group that they were now pitted in the class struggle. Resentments so engendered were revived and aggravated by the Revolution of 1848 and contributed to an attitude wherein even the beneficent acts of the state were viewed with suspicion. The law of 1884, for example, which legalized labor's organized existence, because it required the declaration of significant data concerning leadership, membership, etc., was interpreted in some quarters as a clever subterfuge by which the state was trying to get the syndicats into its power. Legislation concerning incorporation and collective bargaining and even attempts to inaugurate schemes of workers' insurance were received in the same fashion. The Greeks even bearing gifts were not to be trusted.

Aggravating this lack of accord between the workers and the state was the tendency of French labor to resort to violence in its industrial warfare. Given, to begin with, a strongly impulsive temperament and a tendency to belligerence, syndicalist poverty and the absence of strike funds complete a situation making practically impossible those long-drawn-out but relatively orderly trials of endurance that are familiar in the English-speaking world. Under these circumstances strikes to be successful had to be immediately decisive and, in consequence, were fought ordinarily with an abandon which invited or even compelled vigorous government interference. Often, too, the government because of its centralization and the ramifications of its economic activities became itself party to the conflict.

As a result of this general condition of action and reaction the feeling of mutual hostility on both sides grew acute. The government, openly belligerent, imprisoned militant syndicalists, dissolved syndicats, and closed *bourses du travail*. Repeatedly, also, there were threats of state action which went so far as to propose rescinding the law of 1884 and outlawing the whole movement. Particularly irritating to the workers because of its more tangible character was the actual intervention of the government in labor disputes and the giving, either directly or indirectly, of solid aid and comfort to the employers. Thus in the miners' strike of 1906 a state of siege was declared, and more than 20,000 troops were called out and sent into the region affected. Troops fired on the workers during a demonstration at Villeneuve-Saint-Georges in 1908, killing and wounding some of the demonstrators. In the seamen's strike in 1909-1910 the government again actively participated against the workers by replacing the striking seamen out of the navy. In dealing with widespread strikes among its own employees in the post office department at the same time, small concern was shown for the so-called rights of workers.

Climactic among these incidents was the strike which broke out on the railway *du Nord* in October 1910 and almost immediately spread to other lines, including the state railway. The government reaction to this situation was prompt and vigorous. Five of the strike leaders were immediately arrested, and a military emergency was declared. By this action most of the striking workers, as members of the militia, were automatically enrolled in the army, where they were under military orders to desist from their strike activities and to keep the roads in operation. They had no alternative but to accede. It was a high-handed but effective stratagem on the part of the state; in a week the strike was completely broken.

To the workers this particular conflict meant more than a mere defeat at the hands of the state; it represented also, as they saw it, an act of base betrayal. The evil genius who as Premier of France had accomplished their undoing in this instance was none other than their old colleague Aristide Briand, who, as the fiery revolutionist of the eighties, had defended the use of the strike with the same zeal with which he now suppressed it. Already they had seen two of their professed socialist champions, Millerand and Viviani, after having been elevated to the Cabinet, weaned away from their early allegiance. In Briand they had had for the first time a socialist Premier, and with his defection they learned in a final and compelling fashion the utter vanity of reliance on the state or on political conquest.

Thus to original theoretical contentions opposing any political coalition was added convincing practical demonstration that syndicalists must stand on their own feet and progress by their own direct efforts. Political liaison, obviously, was just as futile as it was illogical or inconsistent.

Syndicalist Methods

Having turned their backs on socialist overtures for common action and having thereby renounced all reliance on political methods, the syndicalists were left to struggle on the economic front with the strike as their principal weapon. It, they felt, was never out of season, for, even though unsuccessful, it served a useful purpose, clarifying class lines, widening the breach between capital and labor, and throwing into bold relief the unmistakable presence and character of the class struggle. Strikes were valuable, furthermore, they thought, as preliminary skirmishes preparing the way for that final gesture, the revolutionary general strike, the force on which they placed ultimate reliance and toward which attention was constantly directed.

In the general strike the basic idea revolves around the simple conviction that the proletariat, in order to make its demands effective, "has only to become motionless." The bourgeoisie as a class is thus reduced, as it were, to a state of siege in which, with all production stopped and supplies dwindling, there is no alternative but to surrender.

An idea of long standing, it required the increasing integration of modern industrialism to suggest the possibility of its practical use, and it was not until the discussions of the First Socialist International that it was faced for the first time as a concrete problem of labor policy. Its champion here was the anarchist Bakunin; its antagonist, because it was wholly incompatible with his theory of revolution, was Karl Marx. Introduced into France, it was effectively advocated by Briand before the National

Federation of Syndicats in 1888, and under Pouget's influence it was accepted by the C. G. T. in the decade of the nineties. Here it became an entering wedge of doctrinal difference, resolving revolutionary workers into two distinct groups, one with socialistic, the other with anarchistic conceptions of revolution.

From the Guesdists, upholders of the Marxian faith, came naturally the most vigorous opposition. It was their contention that the indispensable condition of a successful general strike was a degree of organization which, if once achieved, would make unnecessary any resort to such extreme measures, the same result being obtainable in a less drastic fashion. Furthermore the basic contentions were held to be in error. In any trial of economic strength labor is bound to be the weaker party, and, before the employing groups have felt the pangs of hunger, workers will have died of starvation. The general strike was, in short, according to the Guesdists, "general nonsense."

The majority of the syndicalists refused to be moved by these dialectics. The dramatic quality of a general strike had always appealed to their imagination; furthermore, as a revolutionary instrument it offered great tactical advantages. The armed mobs and barricades of the Great Revolution were gone forever. The advance of military science since that day had made such a type of revolutionary effort plainly suicidal. In the general strike, however, they felt they would not fight at so great a disadvantage. By merely refraining from work they could strangle the existing economic system quickly and quietly without exposing themselves in massed fashion, an easy target for the guns of those who were employed to defend it.

This conception of the general strike as a purely passive affair soon gave way, however, as has already been pointed out, to one that was quite different and doubtless

less puerile. This one recognized the improbability that the youthfully vigorous capitalistic regime of France would meekly fold up and surrender itself to a group of striking workers, however unanimous their effort to overthrow or destroy it. Violent reaction from the defenders of the *status quo* was recognized as inevitable. The syndicalist leaders refused, however, to be dismayed at such a prospect. It was pointed out that in the event of a general strike, force, if it were applied by the ruling class, must be applied in such a dispersed fashion, because of industry's wide ramifications, as to make it highly ineffective, leaving the advantage still with the strikers.

As against the practical realism of either of these points of view there arose a tendency, due particularly to the influence of Georges Sorel, to contemplate the general strike not so much as a thing actually to be realized, at least in the present, but rather as a kind of social "myth," a useful abstraction whose moral effect should be considered its most important immediate value. In the interval of waiting while the proletariat was gathering strength to throw off bourgeois control and sound the knell of the capitalistic system, some device must be invented to keep alive the sense of class conflict, to act as a "cloud by day and a pillar of fire by night," keeping the ranks intact and pointed always toward the fulfillment of their ultimate revolutionary purpose. This function, it was felt, the general strike would perform in an effective fashion.

Unhappily, however, so far as the absorption of this point of view by the rank and file was concerned, coincident with the propagation of this "mythical" conception labor disturbances assuming the proportions of general strikes began actually to occur in surrounding countries. It would seem doubtful, therefore, if to the average workman the general strike of the syndicalist movement was ever anything more philosophical or less real than the mob scenes of the Great Revolution, whose memory he venerated and which in this modified fashion he wished to repeat.

While the strike was the principal syndicalist weapon, there was wide resort, also, to the use of sabotage.

Except in a very limited sense this form of industrial warfare is practically taboo among other well-known union movements. If indulged in at all in its more extreme forms, it is used surreptitiously or during times of great stress. The C. G. T., however, at the Congress of Toulouse (1897), contemptuous of the "bourgeois morality" which shrinks from the destruction of property, added it to the repertoire of its official methods of class warfare.

The tendency to lump all forms of interference with production under the title of sabotage, it must be admitted, has made the term almost useless as a basis of distinction or characterization unless it is qualified in some fashion. Obviously, wherever a wage system or an apparent "lump of labor" exists, soldiering, or the nursing of jobs, is inevitable. Such conduct, however, suggests no motive beyond that of a relatively spontaneous, often unconscious attempt at protective adjustments to a given situation. Between this and a conscious and concerted attempt to do little work or bad work or to destroy the employer's property or to take life itself if necessary there is the widest difference. In the first instance we behold, as was stated, merely a protective device, one wholly conservative in its implication. In the second instance the phenomenon becomes distinctly one of class warfare and inspired by a conscious revolutionary purpose.

While the latter conception of sabotage is not wholly exclusive of the former, at least in method, it was to the latter that the syndicalist movement committed itself, presumably without scruple or limit. Thus with sardonic humor Paris barbers shaved the entire heads of customers who asked for service after the hour demanded for closing. Key parts of machinery were destroyed or hidden; crowbars were put in gears, abrasives in bearings; dynamite and other explosives were resorted to, etc.

This undermining of an economic system by the encouragement of bad work or the destruction of property entails for the syndicalist a troublesome and rather obvious dilemma. That which above all else was to distinguish and glorify the syndicalist economic order, once it was established, was its emphasis on production and the dignity of labor, and yet this new era was to come as the climax of years of systematic destruction of capital equipment as well as years of systematic schooling away from good craftsmanship and conscientious effort. This difficulty was relieved in part by placing emphasis on the less destructive and demoralizing practices, such as the "open mouth" methods of clerks, which consisted in merely telling the truth about an employer's merchandise, or the practice among artisans of fabricating with such excessive care that, while the quality was enhanced, costs were raised to such an extent that businesses were ruined. The difficulty, however, could not be wholly relieved in this fashion; consequently syndicalist leaders began gradually to lose their enthusiasm for the whole practice.

The final argument for the rank and file, however, tends to be that of the circumstance, and the determining influence that of expedience. French syndicats were distressingly poor, and, because they were poor, their methods of warfare were limited. Unable to support themselves in the strike off the job, they felt reduced to the necessity of striking on the job, which, granting a revolutionary attitude, means terrorism and sabotage of every variety; and this they continued to practice widely in spite of long-range inconsistencies or leaders' disapproval.

With the same zeal with which the syndicalists strove

to undermine the existing economic system by the use of the strike, sabotage, boycott, etc., they strove, also, to bring to an end French militarism and to eliminate the standing army. The reason for this opposition is apparent. What more reliable defense existed for the present regime than a large mass of paid soldiery? This was the rock on which syndicalism's best-laid plans were going consistently to pieces. During strikes or labor disturbances of any kind it was the army which was always available to cow the workers, even to shoot them down if need be, or to take their places as strike breakers. To add to the anomaly of this situation, the members of the army originally were of necessity largely recruited from among their own number.

Early in the history of the syndicalist movement attention naturally turned to defense against this situation. One of the more systematic attempts, a general assessment known as the *Sou du Soldat*, was for the purpose of rendering financial aid to workers then in the army and of furthering in every possible fashion the conception of fraternity and accord between the workers in industry and those serving, perhaps only for the time being, in the French army.

Nor was this opposition allowed to weaken. In 1905 it found expression in the notorious *Manuel du Soldat*, the most violent and extreme of all syndicalist attacks on the army. This pamphlet in spite of the French government's attempts to suppress it was widely circulated. The following year at the famous Congress of Amiens, at which the general position of syndicalism was restated and clarified, it was resolved that anti-military and anti-patriotic propaganda should be promulgated with the greatest zeal and audacity.

This attitude was maintained to the very eve of the War, when it was climaxed by an agitation against the law which extended the term of military service to three years. This agitation in spite of the tenseness of the international situation was carried to such length as to excite not only the resentment but the fear of the general population, to whom it was nothing short of an incomprehensible and perfidious act of betrayal, that a small minority should thus wilfully seek to undermine the national defense in a time of great national peril.

From the syndicalist point of view, however, there was neither mystery nor treachery involved in this action. On the contrary, since the syndicalists themselves as Frenchmen were susceptible to the same patriotic impulses which motivated their critics, the steadfastness of their anti-militaristic attitude represented an impressive achievement in consistency and loyalty to the syndicalist point of view— a steadfastness soon to give way, however, before the pressure of the War itself. In the meantime they were merely keeping faith with their contention which had always been that the worker has no country and that a patriot without a patrimony is an obvious absurdity.

THE FIRST WORLD WAR AND DEMORALIZATION

Between this uncompromising and revolutionary syndicalism just described and the French labor movement today there is a very wide divergence. With the outbreak of the World War the spirit of the Charter of Amiens began to give way and has to a very large degree been replaced by a mild reformism and a tendency toward class collaboration which approximates the familiar trade union concepts of America. In this transition, furthermore, not only have the revolutionists become a minority group; the very quality of their revolutionary philosophy has shown a tendency to reverse itself. Once the exponents of a modified anarchism, they have largely succumbed to the spell of the Russian Revolution, with its glorification of political activity and the dictatorship of the proletariat.

The War and post-War history of French organized labor becomes, then, largely an inquiry into this change of attitude, the conditions which brought it about, the schisms and secessions that resulted from such a sweeping social realignment, and the nature, also, of the modern or "reformist" point of view.

While no single fact or circumstance may be considered completely responsible for this change, the War itself was so overwhelming and so objective in its consequences as to seem, often, the sufficient explanation. Certain it is that in France as elsewhere the War furnished a convincing demonstration that economic class lines will scarcely remain intact or "mode of production" prevail as the sole determinant of human conduct when these are pitted squarely against that purely "bourgeois" virtue of loyalty to country in times of great national peril.

With Serajevo, the War suddenly changed from a thing of probability to one of impending reality, and the C. G. T. was brought face to face with the most crucial problem of its existence. How, the question was, should it relate itself to France and the existing government in the coming struggle, a struggle which might easily involve not only French national unity but, as they were inclined then to believe, the survival of French national culture as well?

The whole of the past history of syndicalism, it will be recognized, was an irrevocable commitment to one single answer: namely, unyielding opposition to any type of collaboration with the existing state for military purposes but rather a substitution of class lines for national lines and class warfare for the traditional and now existing warfare between nations. Along with the Marxian affirmation "the workman has no fatherland" syndicalism had subscribed always with equal fervor to the injunction "working men of all countries, unite." Such declarations of principle, furthermore, had been supported in a practical fashion by that persistent campaign of opposition to militarism and the French army which had had as its most conspicuous symptoms the *Manuel du Soldat,* the *Sou du Soldat,* and the determined and protracted opposition to the extension of the term of military service in 1913.

In addition to this, past congresses of the C. G. T. had faced the specific issue of the proper conduct of French workers in case a war should actually occur. Thus the Congress of Marseilles in 1908 voted the following resolution:

"The workingmen have no fatherland! in consequence every war is but a crime against the working class, a bloody and terrible method of diverting them from their demands.

"The Congress declares that it must, from the international point of view, educate the workingmen so that in case of war between the powers, the workingmen will respond to the declaration of war by a declaration of a revolutionary general strike."[9]

The position taken at Marseilles was reaffirmed four years later at a special Congress in Paris, when it was declared that should France enter into a war "the duty of every workingman is to refuse to respond to the call to arms and to rejoin his class organization in order to carry on there the battle against his only adversaries: the capitalists."[10] The means designated was the revolutionary general strike.

The government's response to this threat of insurrection at home in the event of war abroad was to direct the police in Paris and throughout the provinces to compile a

[9] M. R. Clark, *A History of the French Labor Movement* (Berkeley, University of California Press, 1930), p. 41.
[10] Léon Jouhaux, *op. cit.,* p. 189.

list of syndicalist leaders and revolutionaries, in order that they might be immediately seized and imprisoned if war actually occurred. This list, known as *Carnet B*, became in turn the cause of increased bitterness in the attitude of the syndicalists toward the state.

Unhappily, however, so far as the syndicalists' heroic position was concerned, doing is seldom so easy as deciding what ought to be done; and the C. G. T., faced finally with the stark reality of an impending German invasion, found itself abandoning its official and oft-repeated attitude with abject precipitation. Jouhaux, the dominant figure and secretary of the organization, when called upon to deliver the funeral oration over the body of Jean Jaurès, instead of seizing the opportunity to condemn the spirit of rampant nationalism that had prompted the assassination, himself spoke in a chauvinistic fashion; and the speech, it must be added, met with general approval. Clearly, even among syndicalists, country for the time was supreme. Class was forgotten.

Considering the hysteria of the moment, for the C. G. T. to have attempted to do otherwise—to have put into operation its oft-repeated threat to forestall national conflicts by interposing the general strike—would have been as foolish as it was bound to have proved futile. Had this been done, declared Merrheim, a leader of the more radical syndicalists, later (1919), "The working class, roused by a powerful current of nationalism, would not have left the task of shooting us to the agents of the government; it would have shot us itself." Another syndicalist leader, Frossard, speaking in the same vein of the wartime policy of the C. G. T., insisted: "The truth is that one does not make a general strike without strikers, that there is no insurrection without insurgents. The truth is that even if we had attempted to apply our congress resolutions, we would have been swept aside by those who, in the mass of workingmen today, tired by the war, reproach us for not having acted in that manner."[11]

During this war, which the syndicalists thus blessed—at least by their acquiescence—the economic life of the country was suddenly reorganized, and all other interests were made subservient to those of military efficiency and national defense. Furthermore, with the exodus of workers into the army, many labor organizations found themselves deprived of most of their membership and thus of most of their vitality. These years exist, consequently, as an interlude of stagnation or even of regression in the physical development of the C. G. T. In the development of a philosophy, on the other hand, they were years of maximum importance.

Once it was conceded that the War was a war of aggression on the part of the Central Powers and that the attitude of the French government was a just one, the obligation to contribute to its successful prosecution was in effect admitted also. The dilemma of the C. G. T. at this point was indeed an impossible one. To have remained aloof or to have attempted an internal insurrection against the War when it was declared would have been, obviously, to have sacrificed the whole syndicalist movement immediately to the war madness of the French people at the moment. On the other hand, to join other existing political and social forces in the common cause of its propagation was to renounce an original heroic position of anti-militarism and aloofness based on fundamental concepts of direct action, the class struggle, and revolution. Once this position was forsaken, it would be difficult to reëstablish, and with its abandonment syndicalism as a separate institution would have lost most of the reason for its continued existence. Thus by the actual seizure of this second alternative, that is, participation in the War, it

[11] M. R. Clark, *op. cit.*, p. 48.

was almost assured that, while the passing of the C. G. T. as a revolutionary force was to be less immediate and less dramatic, it was bound in the end to prove no less inevitable.

This war-time adjustment of the C. G. T., symbolized by an early adherence to the *Union Sacrée* for national defense, found various additional means of expression. Even before the War had actually begun, an accord was sought with the oft-rebuffed Socialist Party, with which it later joined in the creation of the *Comité d'Action*—an accord designed primarily to safeguard workers' welfare and to contribute to "the work of national defense."

Once a breach had been made, the retreat toward complete collaboration became increasingly easy. The more difficult problem, as it later appeared, was to find some means of preserving a face-saving appearance of ultimate loyalty to syndicalist first principles as they were expressed in the Charter of Amiens. Thus without protest Jouhaux was permitted to accept the propagandist government post of *Commissaire à la Nation*, an appointment to the *Comité de Secours National*, which was charged with the relief of destitution occasioned by mobilization, and to the *Commission du Travail*, whose function was the organization of the Paris labor market, etc. Everywhere there were to be found "militants of every rank, from the secretary-general of the C. G. T. down to the secretary of the smallest syndicat, coöperating with their employers on local joint committees."

The doctrine of direct action was scarcely more successfully defended than that of the class struggle. The celebration of May Day, hitherto religiously observed as a symbol of proletarian unity and revolutionary purpose, was almost completely abandoned. Strikes also, which on general principles had been syndicalism's favorite weapon, were no longer encouraged. On the contrary and wholly at variance with syndicalism's most elementary concepts there was a general tendency when trouble threatened to ask for government intervention.

To any recital of this war-time change of policy, carried, it would seem, clearly beyond the demands of protective adjustment to the emergency, it should be added that the government itself assumed a positive role and played no insignificant part. Up to the administration of Clemenceau it had met labor halfway. In contrast to that characteristic attitude of threat and suspicion which had long prevailed, there now appeared tactful gestures of understanding and, repeatedly, of actual helpful cooperation. Thus, to labor, the new-found accord achieved an appearance of genuine mutuality, a thing of common advantage, and, from an opportunistic point of view, of practical good sense. In spite of this, however, as the War grew older and its actual realities became more apparent, the more philosophic and revolutionary began to protest with ever growing bitterness that syndicalism had been betrayed by its war-time leaders.

Reformism

While the War lasted, the problems of syndicalist policy and of the maintenance of syndical unity were relatively simple. Conduct was largely the result of the compulsions of circumstance, and little room was left for opinion or the appeal to principle. A general obsession with the problems of safeguarding the nation made the problems of the individual or the class appear relatively insignificant. As soon as the War was ended, however, this situation became radically altered. The problem of making a living and of personal and class advantage once again became paramount. The C. G. T., now freed from war-time coercions, found itself compelled to stand on its own feet and to defend its policy in terms of inner convictions rather than in terms of a great national emergency.

Considering the general abandonment of syndicalist principles which the War had occasioned, it now became a matter of immediate importance that there be a reappraisal and restatement of these principles in order that the world, indeed, that the syndicalists themselves might know for what the organization stood and whither it was tending. The immediate question was: Should the C. G. T., turning its back on the experiences of the last four years and careless of immediate advantage, now renew its vows to destroy the government with which it had so recently collaborated? Or should it, on the other hand, succumbing to the mellowing influence of those years, become in profession what it had already become in fact—an essentially reformist institution, working both with and through the existing state for the gradual achievement of a better society?

There was no attempt to evade this issue or to delay the answer. On November 24th, "the morrow of the Armistice," at a mass meeting in Paris a program of "minimum demands" was presented to the workers by the central office of the C. G. T. This program, formally ratified in December, reflected the official post-War attitude of syndicalism in much the same manner that the Amiens Charter reflected that which preceded it.

Nothing could have revealed more clearly the permanence of the recent change in syndicalist policy. Pre-War catch phrases were discarded. Instead of resounding affirmations of labor's self-sufficiency, class warfare, and impending revolution there was a painstaking and objective analysis of the affairs of the present, with a cataloguing of those reforms which for the common good demanded immediate realization. Included here were such practical and, in some instances, unorthodox demands as the eight-hour day, creation of a national economic council, social legislation, control of immigration, free trade in necessities, etc. Although the first full congress after the War, that of Lyons the following year, reaffirmed the pre-War position by resolving, "without any possible equivocation, syndicalism declares that it is in its origin, in its present character, and its permanent ideal a revolutionary force,"[12] clearly, the conception of revolutionary method now entertained by the majority had been vastly altered.

While this change has been described in terms of the War alone, it should be observed that the War was not the only force operating in this direction. From a long-time point of view, indeed, it might be reasonably argued that it was not even the most important one, that honor going rather to the Russian Revolution. The War, it will be recalled, in no way discredited syndicalist principles; it merely demonstrated that, as yet at least, indoctrination was not sufficiently thorough to preclude their possible violation. Events in Russia, on the other hand, brought a disturbing uncertainty as to whether these principles themselves might be considered wholly valid. In the face of the serious economic disorganization following the Bolshevist seizure of power, a situation saved only by the importation of bourgeois technicians, bourgeois capital, and a considerable concession to bourgeois methods, what, for example, was to be said of the vaunted contention that the workers were everywhere and always self-sufficient, that, come when it might, the revolution was bound to disclose within the victorious proletariat ability to discharge its new-found responsibilities? Furthermore, while there was, it is true, an impressive confirmation of the syndicalist notion concerning the revolutionary virtues of small

[12] Léon Jouhaux, *op. cit.*, p. 233.

but resolute minorities, the end achieved by that minority was not so reassuring. In contrast to that complete emancipation from authority which the syndicalist contemplated, there actually existed in Russia a relentless dictatorship—not a dictatorship of the proletariat but rather a dictatorship "by a party on the proletariat."

In addition to having this object lesson in the dangers of sudden and violent change, majority opinion of the C. G. T. was influenced, also, by the fact that a minority of their own group, overwhelmed by the mounting prestige of the Bolshevist regime in revolutionary circles, was itself shifting to the Bolshevist point of view. In combating this group and its divisive influence it was only natural that the majority found itself more and more the champion of moderation and gradualness against this opposing appeal to violence and precipitation.

Out of all this evidence and experience the significant conviction which seemed to distill itself and reshape syndical post-War policy was that social revolution lays upon its authors responsibilities as well as privileges. The C. G. T. was now conscious of the fact, insisted Jouhaux, that the revolution will carry with it "not only benefits but also and especially, duties" and that the survival power of the new regime, once achieved, will depend on the capacity of the workers themselves to attain to that mental and moral stature which the responsibilities of their new position require.

With this newer and more sober attitude, syndicalist reaction to social reform was bound to be different. In place of the old hostility to such measures every aid began to be rendered to bring them about. The justification is obvious. Any such legislation was now to be viewed not as a compromise with the existing order but rather as a concession wrested from it. Furthermore and in like fashion it was felt that improvements in the condition of the working class, of whatever origin, were not to be feared as a social opiate, deadening the will to revolt, so much as they were to be sought after as a means to furthering proletarian development, without which the revolution was unthinkable, even though it might be able to be brought about.

As a result of the expansion of such ideas the general strike was discarded as a syndical weapon, and even the industrial strike came to be looked upon with disfavor. The collective agreement was encouraged and the state, once marked for destruction, began to be viewed as a potential ally. The C. G. T., in short, while affirming its fidelity to pre-War revolutionary principles, in its conduct had become at one with the trade unionism of Western Europe—or even with the despised "Gompersism" of America.

SCHISM, AND THE FORMATION OF THE C. G. T. U.

It need scarcely be reiterated that this shift to the right was far from representing the undivided opinion of the entire syndicalist organization. It represented, rather, the majority point of view, entertained by Jouhaux and the central office, the defense of which in the end brought serious internal conflicts and threatened a permanent breach in the unity of the organization.

Underlying this contrary opinion was a strong, almost natural tendency, the prompting of both temperament and tradition, in favor of a more radical conception of revolution. This opposition, assuming at first a purely negative attitude, demanded merely that the C. G. T. keep faith with its pre-War, revolutionary ideals. Later, however, under the spell of Moscow and the Bolshevist example there was a tendency to adopt a more positive attitude and to nudge French labor into the sphere of influence of the Third International. The history of this internal conflict is an intricate one and involves most of the fluctuations of syndicalist conduct and syndicalist fortune from the early years of the War to the formation of a second and rival confederation late in 1921.

The complete unanimity with which the organization forsook its foundation principles to join in the War will be remembered. That, however, was a short-lived accord. By the second year of the War an outspoken group began to be heard in criticism of the majority policy of collaboration. Their contention was, in effect, that, while some concession to the existing emergency was legitimate, there was no occasion for that complete abdication from syndicalist principles which the present conduct of the organization involved.

As the War progressed and the hysteria of 1914 subsided more and more into the war-weariness and disillusionment of the years following, this movement naturally gained in momentum; and by 1917 in spite of attempts to avoid it the burning question of each successive congress was that of the C. G. T. and the War, or, more precisely, that policy of collaboration and reformism toward which the minority grew steadily more bitter and irreconcilable. The prestige of the central office, however, was still overwhelming, while the very violence of the opposition detracted from its effectiveness by estranging those more moderate sympathizers who were still inclined to value syndicalist unity above matters of doctrine. Thus the War came to an end with Jouhaux and the moderates still in complete control.

The tremendous influx into the C. G. T. after the armistice, practically quadrupling its membership, might easily have been interpreted as a vote of confidence in the existing reformist policy and as auguring the approach of a new era of power and stability for the whole organization. Appearances, though, were deceiving. The new members were syndicalists only in name. Not fighters but camp followers, they had joined merely to share in the fruits of syndicalist activity, and what seemed to be a time for general rejoicing was really a time of approaching tribulation out of which the C. G. T. was to come not only a divided but also a discredited institution.

The first attempt at a display of this post-War strength brought also the first serious reversal of fortune. The occasion was that of May Day of 1919. Taking advantage of the widespread unrest that existed among the workers, a nation-wide celebration was carefully planned, partly, it would seem, as a means of increasing labor morale and solidifying the strength of the expanded organization, partly, also, as a demonstration of power designed to hasten the legislation of the "minimum program" demanded at the close of the War, particularly the eight-hour day. For labor it was an auspicious moment, and the day was awaited by all classes throughout France with considerable suspense.

In the provinces the celebration was held without particular interference or significant later consequence. Not so in Paris. The French government, unawed and also unfriendly, at the last moment denied to the demonstrators the use of the streets, thus in effect denying the privilege of the demonstration itself. In the clash which followed there were many casualties on both sides, and a large number of workers were later arrested. In spite of more violent opinion this rebuff was rather meekly accepted, and the event in general became something of an anti-climax from which the C. G. T. emerged considerably deflated.

Following this came a series of strikes which, while largely independent, were so numerous and so widespread as to create the appearance of a concerted attack on the existing social order. Many of these disturbances were the natural product of post-War economic conditions; many, on the other hand, related directly to the feud between moderates and revolutionaries within the C. G. T. and represented a reckless determination on the part of the latter to dominate and to force the whole organization, regardless of majority opinion, into a program of more direct action.

In this latter category was the famous railway strike of 1920, an ill-starred general strike on which the syndical post-War offensive went completely to pieces. Forced by a radical minority, without proper authorization or preparation, and given a revolutionary flavor, its outcome was inevitable and could scarcely have been in doubt from the very beginning. Nevertheless the C. G. T. felt compelled to sanction the idea officially and to join in its propagation.

Successive waves of sympathetic strikers in other occupations were called out until seven of the nation's most important federations were idle, and the whole affair began to look quite imposing. With a determined governmental resistance, however, and a strongly adverse public sentiment attempts to expand the strike beyond this point met with failure, and it began to weaken. On the railways themselves, instead of the anticipated paralysis, essential traffic was kept moving by volunteers. The railway workers were finally forced to yield, and the whole affair ended in failure.

If syndicalist prestige had been damaged by the events of 1919, it was finally and completely demolished by these of 1920. This attempt at a general strike, instead of presenting an arresting demonstration of labor's unity and power, was a betrayal of disorganization and impotence. The immoderate reaction of the government itself reveals the low ebb of syndicalist strength. Of the striking railway workers 22,000 were dismissed and 700 were either imprisoned or otherwise prosecuted; while the C. G. T. itself, only a short time before a thing of power and an object of deference on the part of the state, was now declared to have violated the law of 1884 and to be officially dissolved.

It is somewhat doubtful whether the government could have enforced this decree and actually compelled dissolution. It is likewise doubtful whether it cared to do so, for syndicalism was no longer a thing to be feared. Defeated now and discredited, its membership quickly shrank to the pre-War figure of approximately 600,000.

The net result of these reverses was not merely loss of size and prestige but demoralization and an increase of the bitterness with which moderates and radicals within the organization regarded each other. The air was filled with charge and countercharge as each group discovered in the conduct of the other the cause of its present plight. The successive congresses indicate the progress of this struggle, coming now to its climax.

Reverting to the Congress at Lyons in September, 1919, significant as the first full congress after the War, we observe the majority still secure in its control. The opposition, however, led by the metal and railway workers, basing its arguments on the Charter of Amiens, presented an indictment of the existing policy of reformism and "class peace" with a logic that was devastating. There was no threat of secession as yet but merely a bitter determination, now that the War was ended, to re-commit the C. G. T. to its former militant program. Diplomatically Jouhaux gave promise of a shift in this direction. This gesture of acquiescence together with certain deflections from the minority sustained the majority by a very decisive vote.

Scarcely a year after the Congress at Lyons the C. G. T. was reconvened at Orleans (September, 1920) in an attempt to heal the wounds and ease the tension occasioned by the strikes which had occurred in the interval. Although the relative strength of the two groups had not changed in the meantime, a new institution and with it a new issue had appeared which altered not only the nature of their differences but of their possible outcome as well. This was the communist international trade union movement. The formation of this organization, commonly known as the R. I. L. U. (Red International Labor Union), at once brought to the fore the problem of syndicalist allegiance.

Immediately it became the insistence of the minority that the C. G. T. should forsake the "yellow" Amsterdam International, to which it then belonged, and join the more militant organization centered at Moscow. This the majority resolutely refused to do and, since the R. I. L. U. was demonstrably a creature of the political Communist International, with a good show of reason. By this change of issue, however, the minority achieved a tactical advantage of great importance. It had now a positive unifying appeal in contrast to its former purely negative attitude and was able, furthermore, to enlist in its own behalf the existing wave of enthusiasm for the communist movement. The policy of boring from within, which it now adopted, met with such success that at the instigation of the central office a congress was hurriedly summoned at Lille (July, 1921) to stem the rising tide of its propagandist influence.

This congress marked the climax of these years of growing bitterness and dissension. The debate grew so violent as to compel a resolution in favor of depositing all firearms outside of the assembly chamber. Each side was able to condemn the other in terms of the same classic document—the Charter of Amiens. The minority was accused of betraying the anti-political principles of the

Charter by cleaving to the politically dominated Red International; the majority, on the other hand, was accused of betraying the spirit of the Charter by the adoption of a purely reformist program. Both sides were stubbornly immovable. The vote, due to recent minority successes, was practically equal, and the Congress ended in stalemate.

Although division seemed the only remedy for this situation, both sides were loath actually to bring it about. The minority, influenced by its recent growth, even fostered the hope of shortly becoming the majority and of dictating through sheer strength the policy of the entire organization. Dissolution, though, was at hand. An unauthorized call having gone out for another congress to be held in December, the central office of the C. G. T. issued the ultimatum that all who attended would automatically sever themselves from membership in the central organization. The Congress met, this threat notwithstanding, and in so doing brought the formal unity of the syndicalist movement to an end. The new organization thus automatically created adopted the name *Confédération Générale du Travail Unitaire*, and in form as well as in name was closely modeled after the one from which it seceded.

With the withdrawal of these malcontents the C. G. T. was now free to pursue undisturbed the policy of realism and collaboration which had occasioned all the dissension; so thanks to this division peace came once again to the original organization.

For the seceders, however, the situation was quite different. A survival of the war-time opposition to the nationalism and militarism of the central office, this group was now composed of all who opposed the majority policy for any reason whatsoever and consisted primarily of communists, revolutionary syndicalists, and anarchists, for whom the only unifying fact had been the existence of a common revulsion for syndicalist official War and post-War policy. Freed now from such a unifying emotion and able to proceed in their own fashion, they were at once beset by irreconcilable differences among themselves. All, to be sure, were revolutionists, but for the revolutionary aims of the anarchists, who composed one of the major factions of the seceding group, and of the communists, who composed the other, there could be obviously no common denominator. While the one declared for the destruction of the state and for freedom from all political alliance, the other toiled to make this new organization an extension merely of the Communist International, a political organization under whose influence the union was bound to become a thing of secondary importance.

These differences came to a head at the C. G. T. U. Congress of Bourges in November, 1923. Already the communists had succeeded in squeezing out the anarchists and syndicalists and in monopolizing the positions of authority and influence. Thus they enjoyed an easy triumph in the vote of the Congress itself. Whereupon the dissident groups, the anarchists and revolutionary syndicalists, seceded, and the C. G. T. U. passed completely to communist control. The seceders survived only as a moral influence; as a physical force they ceased to have any further significance in the French labor movement.

All opposition having now been eliminated or stifled in this fashion, the C. G. T. U. dropped every pretense at independence and openly allied itself with the Communist Party. In so doing it submerged itself, its doctrines, and its identity in the international organization to which it now looked for direction and of whose will it became but a local expression. In keeping with this relationship its objective for France became a dictatorship of the proletariat.

Truly the C. G. T. U. had drifted far from the pre-War syndicalism which nurtured it, and the rôle it was now playing compelled sweeping readjustments. To begin with, for the C. G. T. U. to become a creature of the Communist International and to remain at the same time a champion of the syndicalist tradition of local autonomy was obviously impossible; thus the whole administrative scheme was of necessity reorganized. Decentralization and freedom gave way to centralization and control, and authority, formerly generated internally and emanating from the bottom, was now reposed with a foreign institution and sifted itself down from the top. It should be added, however, that in spite of the logical and tactical advantage of this development—independent action and revolutionary force being almost a contradiction of terms —French temperament and habit refused to concede in its practical applications that to which French intelligence had in this manner subscribed. Thus the unions, in spite of official integration, instead of increasing their fighting strength by pooling their financial resources continued to hold them in dispersion; and strikes, instead of reflecting a general plan, the work of a central board of strategy, continued as of old to occur completely at random.

Besides parting from old conceptions of authority, the C. G. T. U. succumbed also to the idea that strength lies in numbers as well as in revolutionary spirit; so in contrast to the old syndicalist contempt for expansion it spared no effort in its propaganda and mass appeal. In keeping also with the general inclination to be dominated by the Bolshevist influence, it discarded the general strike as a final revolutionary weapon and adopted the idea of a civil war, launched at some strategic moment, to effect the downfall of existing society.

The C. G. T. U. Returns to the Fold

To the intransigent revolutionist, who in the face of the steady drift of the C. G. T. toward reformism and moderation found consolation in the staunch inflexibility of this unyielding minority, the subsequent history of the syndicalist movement must bring keen disappointment. Capitalism in France, as elsewhere, as time passed presented to labor an increasingly united front—a fact which made the division of labor's forces an increasingly obvious strategic error. There was, consequently, ever since the breach a persistent effort to re-knit the two branches of the Confederation in the interests of a more effective defense of labor's immediate interests. After some fourteen years of effort this reunion was finally brought about at the Congress of Toulouse in 1936.

This union meant in effect an abandonment by the C. G. T. U. of all that it had stood for and fought to retain. Numbering at that time not more than 250,000, it could be easily dominated in all matters of policy by the 700,000 belonging to the C. G. T. Its course was consequently altered. In accordance with the new circumstance, allegiance, of necessity, was now transferred from the R. I. L. U. back to the International Federation of Trade Unions. While there were indications that this shift probably represented a greater change in letter than in spirit, nevertheless the spirit itself by the evidence of the convention resolutions had undergone considerable alteration. It was voted unanimously that the program for achievement of the reunited group should include among its main items: unemployment insurance, the forty-hour week, minimum wages, collective agreements, the curbing of the power of the capitalistic regime, etc. Last but scarcely least as a gesture confirming the adherence of all groups to the general idea of reformism was the election of Jouhaux to succeed himself as secretary of the organization.

CHAPTER III
GERMANY

Labor under National Socialism

IN JANUARY, 1933, Adolph Hitler became Chancellor of Germany. Among the first institutions to be sacrificed to triumphant National Socialism was the German labor movement in all of its manifestations. Masquerading under the name "socialist" and taking full advantage of the demagogic opportunities offered by the unemployment situation and the feeling of frustration prevailing among the younger members of the working class, this new party was carried to power partly on the shoulders of the laborers themselves.

Once in power, however, its general reactionary nature was quickly revealed, as with characteristic thoroughness it set about to weed out every trace of labor organization, whether political or trade unionist. The Communists, most intransigent of the "Jewish Marxists," as opponents of National Socialism and "betrayers" of Germany were the first to feel the rough weight of this new authority. The trade unions shortly followed. On May 2 their buildings were occupied and their leaders arrested, and on May 13 their entire property was confiscated. While the Social Democrats because of their weak acquiescence—they even voted with the Nazis—might have thought to gain some reciprocation, in that they were disappointed. No quarter was granted, and on June 23 they too were ordered disbanded and their leaders arrested. Therewith an organization formerly of great dignity and potential importance was ingloriously ended. With the destruction of these three institutions the German labor movement, except as it may eke out a precarious and impotent underground existence, became a thing of the past.

Since under the new dispensation the best interests of every class of citizens are presumably safeguarded alike by the state, the state assumes complete control over all industrial relations. This involves conscription of labor and impressment into or out of any occupation as it may suit public policy or the caprice of the controlling power. It involves, also, the denial of any form of collective agreement and the complete domination in industry, as elsewhere, of the totalitarian concept of "full authority downwards; full responsibility upwards."

The Labor Front, a general substitute for all previous organizations, was inaugurated and has been in existence since 1934. In conformity with the National Socialist attitude toward the class struggle the Labor Front is designed to include employers as well as employees. While membership nominally is voluntary, in actuality it is not. Thus the number belonging has become far in excess of the combined membership of all previous labor institutions and extends to approximately 26,000,000. Complex in structure and in function, its primary purpose seems to be that of an agency for effectively mobilizing and propagandizing the German workers.

An important subdivision of the Labor Front is the much publicized "Strength through Joy" movement, German counterpart of the *Dopolavoro* of Fascist Italy. This organization ministers to the general amenity of the workers' lives by such things as sports and entertainment programs and by its widely advertised holiday excursions to points of interest throughout Germany and to neighboring countries. Two million German workers, it is estimated, traveled on this basis within Germany in 1934, while 800,000 more visited neighboring countries. To the onlooker judging superficially, these activities make the new position of the German worker seem rather alluring.

All this, however, is a trifling compensation to the workers for their loss of an independent status and their degradation under the existing regime. It must be remembered, also, that these activities do not in any sense represent a net addition to workers' satisfactions—blessings which flow only from National Socialism. What is now being done ostentatiously by the State in a large measure was already being done quietly but effectively by the workers' own organizations before they were destroyed.

This subjugation of German labor to the whim of a totalitarian political program calls attention again to the drabness of the history of the German working class. Of the various laboring groups in modern civilized countries it was among the last to be delivered from an oppressive medievalism. As an independent social force rendered articulate by its own institutions it was just beginning to make an impact on the German social structure by the end of the nineteenth century. The peak of its influence and prestige was reached in the stormy post-War period and in the early days of the Republic. Failure then to find any common denominator for internal differences, particularly the friction between socialists and communists, is in no small degree accountable for its existing plight. For had these groups been able to weld themselves into a solid front, National Socialism must have been effectively checked.

While it is the hope not merely of friends of labor but of friends of democratic institutions in general that the present eclipse of the German labor movement is a brief interlude in its development, nevertheless, even though the existing situation were to become permanent, German labor organization would remain an object of interest and study. For in spite of the brevity of its history—in some respects, perhaps, even because of it—some of labor's most important problems and tendencies appear with greatest clarity in the German environment. Particularly conspicuous is the play of forces determining labor's ultimate attitude towards the contemporary social order. The direct offspring of revolutionary socialism, German trade unionism, as it groped for some congenial and relatively permanent social attitude, in defiance of the Marxian formula found its way from a radical and doctrinaire position to one of conservatism and practical expedience. The progress of this development is well marked and receives considerable attention in the pages that follow.

Beginning of German Industrialism

The tardiness of a German labor movement is due immediately to the tardiness of Germany's industrial development. So accustomed are we to think of Germany as a great industrial nation, on a par at least with Great Britain, that it is sometimes necessary to be reminded that from the days of Hargreaves, Arkwright, and Crompton in England, almost one hundred years were to pass before the coming of the German Empire and with it the flowering of Germany's industrial civilization.

Among the circumstances responsible for this retardation there might be mentioned first of all the fact that Germany entered the nineteenth century an impoverished country. Possessing a soil that is for the most part infertile, 80 per cent of the people were, nevertheless, still stubbornly devoted to its cultivation. Even the meager prosperity and capacity for capital accumulation which were thus afforded had been sadly interfered with by excessive military activity, for Germany had long been one of Europe's favorite battle grounds.

From an industrial point of view the supply of labor available for work in factories was scarcely more encouraging than the supply of capital seeking investment there. The persistence of rigid medieval restrictions, which applied to both the guild and the manor, by holding workers fixed to traditional occupations or given environments was an effective obstacle to any free labor market.

To this must be added the fact that Germany's commercial possibilities, as well as her economic resources, were extremely limited. Before the coming of the railroad brought an effective means of inland transportation, a landlocked position was an almost insurmountable obstacle to foreign trade, and this obstacle Germany possessed. Furthermore, what was to become the Empire was still, until the decade of the seventies, an agglomeration of independent states, each straining for its own political integrity and private economic advantage. Under such conditions domestic trade suffered almost as much as foreign, for whatever headway was made had to be made against a chaos of types of money, weights and measures, and tariff restrictions.

The tremendous social and economic developments which characterized the nineteenth century, operating within Germany, brought a gradual elimination of her basic difficulties as the century advanced. In 1833 a customs union or *Zollverein* including a group of the leading German states was agreed upon. This brought an end to much of the political and artificial restrictions on domestic commerce. The legal repudiation of the economic caste system which had prevailed in agriculture since the medieval period, beginning early in the century, was almost completed by 1850. Through this change agricultural labor was now enabled not only to move from place to place but to engage in any occupation it might choose to enter. This same period saw, moreover, the breaking down of the guild restrictions of the cities. There *Gewerbefreiheit* (freedom to choose and enter any occupation), a type of freedom that existed nowhere in Germany before 1808, by the middle of the century had become almost universal. Throughout this period, consequently, a "frozen" labor supply was being made more and more available, and a significant obstacle to economic progress thus eliminated. Almost identical with the *Zollverein* in time of occurrence was the beginning of German railways. These, by their coming, to a very considerable degree lifted from Germany the original curse of a landlocked position and consequent trade isolation. Internally, also, they made the *Zollverein* significant, inasmuch as they made physically possible that local exchange which this unifying legislation had been designed to promote.

By 1850, then, the physical basis of German industrialism had been fairly and definitely established. Aided, doubtless, by the acquisitions, both in money and territory, of the Franco-Prussian War and the stimulating and integrating effects of the coming of the Empire, the last quarter of the century found Germany in full career on a program of industrial expansion unprecedented both in its scope and in its rapidity.

In spite of the swiftness of this change, however, German labor was less victimized by the German industrial revolution than English workers had been long before by corresponding changes in their own country. The Germans had the English experience before them, a thing from which they could profit. They were relieved of the necessity, which the British had faced, of groping for both an effective industrial technique and simultaneously for a social environment in which that technique might successfully function. A foreign technology was appropriated in a relatively mature form and superimposed with the minimum of friction and disorganization upon an existing social structure. The problem of labor displacement in particular, so acute in England, was rendered less severe by the fact that industrialization came not as an alternative to handicraftism but rather as an addition to the prevailing agricultural life, thereby expanding the total of the employment opportunities. Nevertheless it was impossible that changes so fundamental could be made without some disorganization and upheaval. The impact, of course, was upon the craftsmen and was localized. It was confined largely to Prussia and Silesia, centers for the manufacture of cotton and woollen cloth by the old handicraft method. Here the violence of the uprisings of the workers affected bore testimony to the seriousness of the local problem of labor adjustment. Government interference occurred with characteristic promptness and vigor —not to relieve the conditions, merely to quell the disturbances.

It should not be assumed, however, that, because German workers were spared the complete uprooting which brought tragedy to the craftsmen of England, their lot was therefore a happy one. On the contrary conditions both political and economic had long been in conspiracy against them. In attempting to explain the remarkable response of the workers to Lassalle and his bizarre theories of social reform in the decade of the 1860's, Kirkup wrote as follows: "It would be easy to ridicule the enthusiasm for Lassalle entertained by these workmen on the Rhine, but it will be more profitable if we pause for a moment to realize the world-historic pathos of the scene. For the first time for many centuries we see the working man of Germany aroused from his hereditary degradation, apathy, and hopelessness. Change after change had passed in the higher sphere of politics, one country after another had traversed the Rhine countries, but, whoever lost or won, it was the working man who had to pay with his sweat and toil and sorrow. He was the anvil on which the hammer of these iron times had fallen without mercy and without intermission."[1]

[1] Thomas Kirkup, *A History of Socialism* (London, A. and C. Black, 1913), p. 89.

In attempting any rationalization of the rise of the German working-class movement it will be useful to remember that, although the Germany of those days was still an agglomerate of 26 independent states representing people of differing cultures, political traditions, and economic environments, there were some experiences of a significant quality which were quite common to them all. From the cradle to the grave, life for most of these people had been dominated for generations by legal and traditional prohibitions and controls. Autocratic governments with strong paternalistic tendencies reached down to determine many of the minute details of their daily lives. Strict guild regulations, also, and manorial customs which found their origin in medieval days survived well into the nineteenth century and narrowly circumscribed their social and economic life. For many of them, too, the presumption in favor of regularity and conformity which such conditions would tend to promote was intensified by the disciplining, regimenting influence of four years in the German army.

While it must be admitted that from an employer's point of view the human product thus created became the almost perfect adjunct of a machine civilization, it failed by that same token to present a fertile field for the spontaneous occurrence of workers' organizations. Even the ancient tradition of master and journeyman and apprentice, for instance, with a clear line of cleavage between them, could not be put off like a cloak, and, while it remained, attempts at unionization obviously were bound to be much impeded.

It seems perfectly natural, therefore, that even after a wage system was finally established, organization hesitated to make its appearance. Other things being equal, it seems just as natural that the beginning of that movement, when it did come, should be quite at variance with the same phenomenon in our own country. Here in America a tradition of individualism and democracy naturally found expression in the world of labor in spontaneous independent action. In Germany an equally strong tradition of submission and dependence operated to make orders and central authority prerequisite to the origination of any new institutions or significant group activity. Indeed, to anyone familiar with the dominant social psychologies of the two countries it must appear as a matter of course that our labor movement should have sprung up almost at random, without strong centralizing influence or dominant authority, and that centralization should have come by a process of amalgamation and should represent a relative degree of maturity. On the other hand, equally consistent with the German environment was the tendency demonstrated by German workers to wait for leadership and the tendency also for both the movements and their philosophies to expand from a single nucleus or to emanate from a given center.

BEGINNING OF THE MODERN LABOR MOVEMENT; COÖPERATION; THE HIRSCH-DUNCKER UNIONS

Because of the social conditions in Germany and the general psychology of German workers a working-class movement failed to spring up with immediate and widespread spontaneity as industrialism developed. When it did occur, it displayed as many strands as there were sources of significant leadership. These workers' institutions together with their forerunner the German coöperatives will now be examined.

Exclusive of the so-called yellow unions[2] and the inde-

[2] The yellow unions were really not trade unions at all after the traditional conception. On the contrary they were quite similar to the "welfare" unions of our own country, founded and subsidized by the employers. At the outbreak of the War they had a membership of approximately 300,000; with the withdrawal of employer support after the revo-

pendent unions, neither of which played an important part in the shaping of German trade union history, the organized labor movement as it passed into the hands of the National Socialists in 1933 was composed of three separate and, in a sense, competing institutions. Foremost among these by a very wide margin, both in size and in general social significance, were the Free unions, offspring of and politically continuously identified with Germany's Social Democratic (socialist) Party. Of much less importance were those unions founded almost simultaneously (the decade of the 1860's) but constructed after the British model and known as the Hirsch-Duncker unions. The Christian unions were of a somewhat later origin (the decade of the 1890's) and drew their membership largely from the Roman Catholic Church.

Antedating the beginnings of modern trade unionism in Germany was an experimentation with coöperation. The history of this movement furnishes so significant a part of the controversial background of the socialist movement and thus indirectly of trade unions that the latter is difficult to discuss without some preliminary reference to coöperation as well.

This movement began with a credit society founded in 1850 by Herman Schulze of Delitzsch. Its immediate occasion was a lamentable dearth of credit facilities for the poorer classes of people, who were being mercilessly exploited by loan sharks. While it was the wish of Schulze that the movement should widen its scope to include producers' and consumers' coöperatives as well, the first years of coöperation in Germany were very disappointing. The seemingly insuperable obstacle was the attitude of the

---

lution and the denial of representation in the National Economic Council and similar bodies this number decreased. Survival capacity, however, was not wholly lacking, and in 1925 they still had 250,000 members.

workers themselves, the people for whose benefit primarily the whole program was being established. Unfortunately for coöperation these workers, while yet unorganized, were falling rapidly under the sway of certain socialist intellectuals who not only resented the bourgeois flavor of coöperation, and credit coöperation in particular, but were inclined to hold all attempts to improve the condition of the laboring class within the framework of the existing capitalistic society to be mere temporizing and tinkering and predestined to failure. Chief instigator of this socialist opposition was Ferdinand Lassalle, whose activities in connection with the founding of the socialist movement and of the Free or socialist trade unions made him one of the outstanding personalities in German labor history.

In turning now to the rise of trade unionism it should be remembered that, while Prussian workers were no strangers to organization back in the days of the flourishing journeyman's guilds, these guilds had been almost completely destroyed by the General Prussian Code of 1794, an act of suppression that was further supported by the Industrial Code of 1845. Since the Prussian situation typified that which prevailed throughout the German states, it may fairly be maintained that throughout the first half of the last century organization of any kind was practically non-existent and that not until the revolutionary period of 1848 were there any significant attempts to resort to concerted action. During that time of general upheaval some associations were formed and a few collective agreements were made. This activity, however, was confined principally to printers and tobacco workers and was destined to be brief and inconsequential. In general neither employers nor employees had much enthusiasm as yet for such methods of regulating industrial conditions, and the whole movement was swallowed up in the period of reaction that followed after the revolution had ended.

The decade of the 1860's saw the abolition, first in Saxony and later in Prussia, of the laws against combination, and therewith began the first general movement toward labor organization.

Almost simultaneously, under the influence of this new freedom two opposing forces reached out to quicken the still inert mass of German labor and to beckon it in diametrically opposing directions. On one side was Max Hirsch, a German liberal and social reformer steeped in the individualistic philosophy of a laissez-faire England. Committed to the support of the existing economic and political regime, he asked only that the workers be allowed to organize in order that they might pursue their own best interests within it. Opposed to Hirsch was the socialist Ferdinand Lassalle, who, flouting the possibility of any fundamental improvement of labor's condition under the existing capitalistic system, sought immediately to inspire the workers to assert themselves politically and to bring about its overthrow. Thus from the beginning German labor found itself rallied into two opposing camps: one, laissez faire, devoted to the concept of the ultimate harmony of interest between capital and labor, the adequacy of self-help, the beneficence of the existing order, and the undesirability of political action; the other, propagating the gospel of class struggle, the futility of self-help, and the necessity for the seizure of political power in order to bring about a social revolution.

It was quite natural that Hirsch, preferring as he did the English social point of view, should have had a prejudice also in favor of English social institutions. Accordingly, when in 1868 he wrote his "Workers' Letters," recommending united action, he described the English model of trade unionism and urged its desirability for

German adoption. The fruit of his efforts was the formation of the *Gewerkvereine* or Hirsch-Duncker unions.[3] The event which actually projected Hirsch into the now rapidly growing factional struggle to organize German labor, largely, it would seem, as a means of furthering the private ends of the different doctrinal groups engaged in its cultivation, was a congress of Lassalleans which convened in Berlin in September, 1868. Aware that this convention was being called for the express purpose of sponsoring a trade union movement under the egis of Lassalle's budding socialist party, its anti-union tradition and contentions notwithstanding, Hirsch made a desperate effort to outsmart its leaders and to win the assembled delegates away from socialist influence. It was his hope, obviously, to lure the whole embryonic union movement into the "backwater" of the Progressive Party, where ultimately it would be organized, he hoped, on a more conservative basis. His failure to gain a hearing, followed by his forcible ejection from the meeting itself, made some sort of retaliation inevitable; its form, naturally, was that of his own independent organizing activity and his own type of unions.

With the help of that perspective which the lapse of years now makes possible, it seems that it should have been easy to predict that an institution shaped, as was Hirsch-Duncker unionism, to accord with the philosophy of British liberalism could scarcely find in the Germany of that day an appropriate environment and that to start

[3] Franz Duncker, whose name, hyphenated with that of Max Hirsch, is used to distinguish this particular type of union organization, was a German politician, labor leader, and journalist of liberal inclination. He warmly supported Schulze-Delitzsch in his attempts to start a coöperative movement. With Hirsch he held to the idea of a unity of interest between capital and labor and opposed with him the socialist contention that the ultimate purpose in the formation of trade unions was the furtherance of the class struggle, the hastening of a social revolution, and the formation of a socialist state.

such a movement would be something of a misadventure. At all events, the organization did not flourish. Its philosophy of individualism, self-sufficiency, and self-help was not, as we have indicated, the philosophy of the German workers to whom it must make its appeal. And while its thoroughly innocuous character from both a political and economic point of view won for it complete exemption from the anti-socialist laws that later bore so heavily on its socialist rivals, the Free unions, even this advantage could not compensate for the fundamental misfortune of a general lack of harmony with its German surroundings. Scorned by the more heroic Free unions, the Hirsch-Duncker unions, while able to survive, were never able to exert any great influence over the quality of Germany's working-class movement. At the peak of their expansion (1922) they were able to claim the relatively insignificant total of only 231,000 members.

Socialist Influence; Lassalle and the Formation of the Universal Workingmen's Association

In contrast to this inability of the Hirsch-Duncker unions to make progress was the impressive success of the Free unions. Indeed, so completely did the latter come to dominate the field that the history of German trade unionism can neither be discussed nor understood apart from the history of their fostering parent, the socialist movement, or more precisely the Social Democratic Party, of which for years they were an integral part and with which to the end they remained closely allied.

Differing, as this does, so strikingly from our own American experience, it may not be inappropriate to reiterate that considering their background it should not seem unnatural that the doctrine to which German workers proved most responsive was one which magnified the beneficent possibilities of the state. Neither is it unnatural that they should draw from that doctrine the obvious corollary that the most effective strategy on their part would be the seizure of political power in the state, in order that it might be made the effective instrument of their own relief. This was the very essence of the appeal of the new socialist movement then rising in Germany, particularly as it was being interpreted to the workers by its most powerful and colorful advocate, Ferdinand Lassalle.[4]

European socialism of the beginning of the century, inasmuch as it was dominated by the modern Utopians, had been French or English in its origin, anarchistic in its tendency, and middle-class in its appeal. The new or "scientific" socialism now appearing in its stead, conceived by Rodbertus, Marx, Engels, and Lassalle, was German in its origin, political in its outlook, and addressed distinctly and exclusively to the working class. And regardless of whether it was to be interpreted as fructifying immediately in the state workshops or coöperatives of Lassalle or ultimately in a dictatorship of the proletariat, toward which, according to the Marxian formula, society unerringly gravitated, this new doctrine was featuring what the German mind was prone to emphasize.

The complete dominance of Marx in the early international socialist movement tends to obscure the fact that in Germany itself socialism owes its origin and much of

[4] Ferdinand Lassalle (1825-1864) was a brilliant and ambitious Jewish intellectual and man of affairs. He rose to a position of some social prominence as the legal champion of the Countess Hatzfeldt. This relationship colored his whole career. Like Marx he was an Hegelian, but unlike Marx he refused to discard the German idealistic philosophy for a materialistic approach. He refused also to accept the idea of the class war and turned his attention rather to the possibilities of State Socialism and so became one of socialism's most important political pioneers.

Curiously enough, although the would-be emancipator of the working class, he was a lover of luxury and high society. A product of this phase of his activity was an unhappy love affair which led to a duel costing him his life, just as his reform movement was getting fairly started.

its early outlook to Lassalle, the "Wunderkind" of his generation of agitators and social reformers.

In 1862, already prominent through the part he had played in the political controversies then raging, he was seized by the Prussian police and charged with being an insurrectionist. The trial which followed, while not acquitting him of the charge, added greatly to his prestige as an opponent of existing political and economic conditions. The next year, therefore, when a body of workers at a convention in Leipzig, dissatisfied with the existing political parties then bidding for their support, began to discuss the advisability of forming a party of their own, they turned to Lassalle for advice.

The Open Letter (March 1, 1863) in which he replied is an historic document. It is at once a clear statement of his own conception of an appropriate political program for labor and at the same time the symbol of the embryonic beginning of German Social Democracy.

The history of the human race, maintained Lassalle, has been a history of struggle for freedom from the enslaving influence of an unyielding physical environment and all the ills with which man has been forced to reckon. In this struggle nothing could be more apparent than that isolated individual effort is impotent and futile. Only through unity of action had society progressed, and the highest and most effective form of unity exists in the state itself. It is through its agency, therefore, that man will achieve his highest development.

From such a premise there issued but one clear course of action for the workers to whom it was addressed, and that was to gain control of the state and to make of it the potent instrument within their own hands of effecting their own economic salvation. Against the Manchestrian conception of freedom and individualism with which the Liberals sought to indoctrinate labor, Lassalle protested, insisting that such a laissez-faire philosophy was defensible only in a society where all were equally rich or equally intelligent; but that, where these elements of power were not equally apportioned, liberty became merely license within which the strong were made free to prey upon the weak.

Since equal suffrage for the German workers was the first step in such a program, it became the immediate goal, in his estimation, for the worker's achievement. Following that—the end for which suffrage was merely the means—would be the elimination of the capitalist employer and with him the surplus value or profits which he appropriated. To this end Lassalle proposed to replace the existing economic organization of society with a vast system of workers' coöperatives to be financed and maintained by the state. Through these coöperatives workers, having become their own employers, would of necessity reap the entire product of their efforts, and thus capitalistic spoliation would be forever effectively ended.

Having seized upon this expedient, however, Lassalle found himself at once coming to grips with Schulze-Delitzsch, whose efforts in the cause of workers' coöperation have been already recited. Agreed as to the institution, namely, coöperation, these two aspiring labor leaders disagreed as to the manner in which it should function. The issue was both clear-cut and ancient. On the one hand was the socialist contention that the poverty of the workers was such that coöperation in order to be sufficiently inclusive to become effective must be a state enterprise which the workers should make their own through a seizure of political power. Opposed to the Lassallean conception of the importance of the state to labor was the laissez-faire doctrine that labor was a free agent and capable of working out its own salvation by its own independent efforts and that any interference on the part of the state was not only unnecessary, it was also unwise.

Against Schulze and this latter concept of labor self-sufficiency, Lassalle now invoked the old Ricardian theory of wages, refurbished and presented as the "iron law."

"The iron economic law," said he, "*which, in existing circumstances,* under the law of supply and demand for labour, determines the wage, is this: that the average wage always remains reduced to the necessary provision which according to the customary standard of living, is required for subsistence and for propagation. . . . It cannot permanently rise above this average level, because in consequence of the easier and better conditions of the workers there would be an increase of marriages and births among them, an increase of the working population and thereby the supply of labour, which would bring the wage down to the previous level or even below it. On the other hand, the wage cannot permanently fall below this necessary subsistence, because then occurs . . . a diminution of the number of workmen caused by their misery, which lessens the supply of labour, and therefore once more raises the wage of the previous level."[5]

The only way actually to improve the condition of the laboring class, he reasoned, was to free it from the existing economic system from which alone the iron law derived its validity. Furthermore the only way to escape from this system must be through state intervention in labor's behalf, for, as previously stated, poverty stood as the insuperable obstacle to the independent achievement of that all-embracing system of coöperation which from the Lassallean viewpoint was capitalism's only available substitute.

To Lassalle's argument it may obviously be retorted, parenthetically, that, if by pooling their resources work-

[5] Kirkup, *op. cit.*, pp. 103-104.

ers through coöperatives should become their own employers through their own efforts, they must of necessity enjoy the entire return from their labor. More than this they could not do under any alternative condition, state socialism of the Lassallean variety or otherwise. Lassalle's case against Schulze, then, as based on a theory of wages, seems rather artificial and empty.

Regardless of the intrinsic merit of this argument, however, it helps at least to betray the total lack of appreciation on Lassalle's part of the possibilities of trade unionism and the collective agreement. Both sides, in fact, were seeing the labor movement wholly through the eyes of the intellectual, of whom Lassalle is historically one of the purest examples. Through this controversy it is made quite clear that his domination of the German labor movement would have meant the ascendence of a philosophy particularly contemptuous of the trade union. For to him it and all kindred devices for resolving the labor problem within a society dominated by the iron law of wages must be equally worthless.

The tangible results of the Open Letter and of Lassalle's subsequent vigorous agitation was the formation at Leipzig in 1863 of the Universal Workingmen's Association, the organic beginning of the Social Democratic Party.

Reflecting precisely the will of its founder, this organization adhered to the idea of a complete separation from the Liberal Party and a repudiation of its economic doctrines of individualism and the adequacy of self-help. In its scheme of organization it was a highly centralized and autocratic institution, complete authority and responsibility resting with the president. This of course was all very well so long as Lassalle himself was available for that office. But by this very fact his death, scarcely more than a year after the association was founded, was the more disastrous. The movement was still in its infancy; its 4,610 members had no experience in organized action, and there was great need for stimulation and effective control. In Bernhard Becker, Lassalle's successor, the qualities of leadership which Lassalle possessed were conspicuously lacking. Following the death of Lassalle the man most capable of directing the affairs of the Association was not Becker but J. V. von Schweitzer, editor of the *Social Democrat*. Although unacceptable at first because of his reputed immorality, by 1867 the Association was in such a plight that he was made president, this obstacle notwithstanding. The damage, however, had already been done. By the interlude of incompetent leadership the growth of the Association was permanently arrested.

Marx versus Lassalle

As compared to the self-help idea of relief incorporated in the Hirsch-Duncker unions or in the coöperative schemes of Schulze-Delitzsch the Lassallean organization, with its political and revolutionary emphasis, had an obvious margin of advantage. More than either of these it fit into its environment and found itself in conformity with the social psychology of the working people at that time. The real threat to the domination of the Lassallean organization was to come from another quarter. It was due to the appearance of an antagonist within its own socialistic household, speaking its own language, and relying essentially on the same type of appeal. This antagonist was the international socialist movement under the leadership of Karl Marx, who as an exile from Germany was then living in London.

Neither the theories of Lassalle nor his tactics met Marx's approval. Holding, as he did, to an evolutionary and deterministic concept of human society and contemplating, consequently, its gradual systematic unfolding in accordance with immutable economic law, Marx resented the short-cut methods of Lassalle as superficial, illogical, and subversive. In spite of Lassalle's persistent attempts to win Marx's friendship, approval, and support, persistent advance met with equally persistent rebuff. Marx's jealous disposition was unable to tolerate the slightest deviation from the narrow path of his own doctrine.

One specific theoretical difference between the two was based on the iron law of wages.[6] Made, as we well know, the cornerstone of the Lassallean defense against Schulze-Delitzsch and his scheme for coöperation, this law was an obvious contradiction of an equally basic contention of Marx; namely, the familiar concept of increasing misery. If the iron law stood as an effective barrier to any increase in labor's wages, by the same token it had a very definite negative beneficence in that it was just as incapable of yielding to any tendency toward their diminution. In contrast to this, the Marxian approach to wages was one of unrelieved pessimism. In a capitalistic society, so Marx reasoned, profits (surplus value) extracted from labor flow invariably into the expansion of capital equipment (constant capital). This process has as its necessary sequel overproduction, the progressive technological displacement of labor itself, and the expansion of the unemployed "reserve army." The forces operating here work with cumulative intensity until there is achieved that condition

[6] It is not easily apparent how the iron law, which in its origin was not a subsistence theory but rather a theory based on customary standards of living, could be made a complete logical defense against either coöperation or trade unionism. According to Ricardo, whose reasoning Lassalle adopted, the "friends of humanity" wish primarily for a sharpened "taste for comforts and enjoyments," that is an elevation of the standard of living. There seems to be no reason a priori why either coöperation or trade unionism might not contribute to this particular end.

Against the Marxian conception of progressive labor degradation it was vulnerable also. As labor grows more demoralized through increasing unemployment, it will be compelled to acquiesce to ever lower standards of living and thus, according to Lassalle's own reasoning, to an ever declining level of wages.

of complete despair and degradation out of which inevitably and ultimately must come social revolution, the "birth pangs" of a new order.

The attempts to magnify the importance of the existing state, the right of suffrage and political conquest, and the potentialities of producers' coöperation, however glorified, Marx held in no higher esteem than the iron law of wages as Lassalle envisaged it. By his own formula salvation was to come only through the operation of broader, more imponderable forces. All this experimentation was but chasing after shadows and bound to end in disaster.

In the conflict between these two men, each bidding for the messiahship of Germany's incipient working-class movement, whoever lost or won, a socialist intellectual would obviously be in the saddle. What, then, it may reasonably be asked, in terms of the fortunes of that movement did it all signify? The answer lies in the difference in the attitude of the two men towards trade unionism.

In contrast with Lassalle's purely intellectual approach and his profound contempt for all such institutions as the trade union Marx has fairly been called a "narrow trade unionist." Time and again he conceded the importance of the union as a desirable, even indispensable, instrument through which workers ultimately were to achieve their revolutionary triumph. This general attitude is made quite clear in the oft-quoted conversation with Hamann of the German Metal Workers' Union: "The trade unions are schools of socialism. . . . All political parties . . . without exception . . . arouse in workers but a passing enthusiasm; the trade unions, however, grip the laboring masses for good. . . . They only are capable of realizing a true labor party and of offering a bulwark of resistance to capitalism."[7]

[7] Quoted from Selig Perlman, *A Theory of the Labor Movement*, p. 77. Cf. also A. Lozovsky, *Marx and the Trade Unions* (New York, International Publishers, 1936).

Regardless of the quality of the abstract logic of these two opponents, however, Lassalle within Germany was able to appeal much more powerfully to the German people than was Marx from his place of exile. Lassalle's last journey through the industrial districts of the Rhine valley is described by Kirkup as comparable to a "royal progress on a triumphal procession." Had he lived, his indigenous state socialism with no place for trade unions doubtless would have dominated revolutionary thinking in Germany and become the goal of its working-class aspirations.

Development of Marxism and the Union of the Two Factions

Scarcely had Lassalle's death occurred, however, before the Marxians began to make definite encroachments on this field of his cultivation. Two institutions were particularly responsible for the spread of Marxian influence. One was the First Socialist International (1864-1876), which Marx dominated. The other was that of the *Arbeiterbildungsvereine* or Workers' Educational Associations of Germany.

While the International was never able to boast of a strong following in Germany, its outposts there served as a very convenient base for propaganda. The educational associations, on the other hand, were a numerous, purely indigenous type of organization which sprang up over Germany in this period of revival and development. Partly as a defense against government suspicion and interference they were led to adopt their disarming title. They were, in fact, more social than political and were described as "searching for a policy rather than possessing one." With the rise of Lassalle and his Workingmen's Association many of the former, particularly those in South Germany, still detesting Prussian institutions merely because they were Prussian, became interested primarily in defending themselves against this new organization and its mounting influence.

Here, surely, was opportunity fairly bursting the door for Marx and his international socialists, a situation which they were not long in reducing to their advantage. The men primarily responsible for the conquest of these educational organizations and their successful delivery into the Marxian fold were those two immortals of German Social Democracy—William Liebknecht and August Bebel.

Liebknecht, coming from the learned middle class of Germany, had taken asylum in London after the collapse of the Revolution of 1848. There he fell under the influence of Marx and became one of his most devoted disciples. In 1861 Liebknecht's return to Germany was made possible by the general political amnesty declared in honor of Emperor William I. Back in Germany, as a member of the staff of the *North German Gazette* he began to try to deflect the rising Workingmen's Association in the direction of Marx and the International.

Led by hatred of Bismarck's statecraft, he resigned his position when he discovered that the *Gazette* was under the Chancellor's influence and was thereupon promptly expelled from Prussia. In Saxony, where he sought refuge, he came in contact with August Bebel.

Although Bebel had familiarized himself with Lassalle's teachings in order to combat his influence more effectively, as yet he knew nothing of Marx, who, thanks to his exile, was still practically unknown to the workers of his native Germany. Under Liebknecht's influence, however, Bebel's original conservatism, already much damaged by the Lassallean arguments he strove to refute, rapidly gave way, and he was soon made the chief apostle of Marxian socialism in South Germany. This conversion of Bebel was a signal victory for the Marxians, for so thoroughly did Bebel dominate the educational associations of this area that they were now easily drawn with him into the socialist camp. In 1869 these groups with seceders from the Workingmen's Association and other less significant bodies organized themselves at Eisenach into the Social Democratic Labor Party.

The program adopted by this new organization was thoroughly Marxian, concessions being made to the Lassalleans sufficient only to avoid the possibility of forever precluding any amalgamation of the two groups. Thus three organizations, one liberal, the Hirsch-Duncker unions, and two socialist, Marxians and Lassalleans, now existed in Germany, each claiming to preach the true gospel and each aspiring to the supremacy of the labor movement.

The general plot as it affected trade unionism now began to unfold rapidly. That Berlin convention of Lassallean socialists (adherents of the Workingmen's Association) which as a by-product and in the manner already described precipitated the Hirsch-Duncker union movement, had as its conscious and considered product a plan to organize labor into 33 groups each of which was to be represented by a trade union. Of this number 9 were immediately organized, and at their first national congress held a year later at Cassel 11 unions with a membership of 35,200 were represented. The entire membership of the organization had grown to approximately 50,000.

But in spite of this very satisfactory progress an apparently incredible thing now happened. Seemingly without warrant or warning the whole movement was uprooted and recast in a different mold, this time without any consideration for trade distinctions and in such a fashion as to make for the complete domination of the unions by the parent organization, the Socialist Party.

Nothing could have revealed more clearly the lack of good faith on the part of its sponsors nor have demonstrated much more effectively the reasonableness of labor's almost universal and abiding distrust of the intellectual. For to these professional reformers too often, seemingly, the thing of final importance is the symmetry of a "system" or the integrity of a theory, and whatever contribution is made to labor's immediate and conscious needs and desires is in the nature of a by-product to be conserved or sacrificed as policy or conceptions of consistency may happen to dictate.

The explanation of this particular incident is simple and throws some light on the general situation. It lies in the fact that in spite of Lassalle's known attitude toward trade unionism his successor, von Schweitzer, felt compelled to yield to the demands of the circumstance. Labor, it appeared, was more sensitive to the appeal of trade unionism than to that of any other alternative device; moreover this was the method that others angling for labor's support were adopting. This concession, however, proved wholly intolerable to those for whom the Party existed primarily to perpetuate in its original purity the point of view of its founder, Lassalle. To the unyielding opposition of this group, led by that same Countess Hatzfeldt who had played so large a part in Lassalle's early life, trade unionism under the fostering care of the Association was virtually sacrificed. The movement was as yet too tender to withstand the shock of such heroic treatment. The presidents of four of the leading unions immediately resigned, and a decline set in from which there was no recovery.

The unionizing activity of the Marxian opposition, the "*Eisenachers*," under the leadership of Bebel was more successful. Although the Eisenach Congress (1869) had included no resolutions definitely creating such organizations, it had given definite support to the idea. To the realists of this group it seemed perfectly clear that workers could scarcely be appealed to nor their loyalty successfully established by anything so doctrinaire as the Marxian formula, assuming even that it could be made intelligible. Philosophic concepts of the ultimate, it was felt, had to be bolstered by some concessions to the needs of the hour. This point of view was neatly expressed by the *Volksstaat*, official party organ, as follows: "By far the greater number of working men have no fancy for attempting anything by way of politics. Besides they are not easily aroused. They are most accessible to such points as increased wages, shorter hours, sick and traveling funds. This thoroughly practical bent of the working class must be turned to account by those who know and have experienced that industrial organization is naturally and historically the chosen instrument for helping labor gradually to supremacy." It is difficult to refrain from adding that this bit of hardheaded realism has more than a local implication; it might be contemplated with profit by all those who see in the laboring man an incipient revolutionist.

Little time was lost in converting these expressed convictions into practical realities, and unions after the English model were quickly established. They grew slowly, however, and for more than a decade were almost devoid of industrial importance.

After the launching of this union movement by the Marxians the next important step in the working-class development became the unification of the socialist parties. For after Eisenach, as we now realize, Germany had two socialist organizations, Lassallean and Marxian, each prompted by the same motives, pursuing essentially the same policy and facing the same opposition, but each at the same time fighting the other. This struggle of socialists became the struggle also of trade unionists, in as much as trade unionists were socialists, and thus both movements were being blighted by the same unfortunate circumstance. Happily this condition came to an end in 1875 at Gotha, when the two groups sank their separate identities to form the modern Social Democratic Party. With the confluence of these two streams, one originating in Leipzig in 1863, the other in Eisenach in 1869, the way was prepared for a more successful development of the entire labor movement in both its political and its economic aspects.

Bismarck's[8] Attack on the Socialists and the Development of the Trade Union Point of View

A new type of disaster, however, was now rapidly approaching. Almost from the beginning Bismarck had viewed the rise of a German socialist party with apprehension and disfavor. Not only did it flout most of the aims he hoped so dearly to accomplish; many of its members even spoke openly of the desirability of a social revolution. A general and unconcealed sympathy with the Paris Commune in 1871 was to him the final, convincing bit of evidence that the welfare of the young Empire demanded the extermination of the Social Democratic Party. After unsuccessful negotiations looking toward united anti-socialist action on an international basis a con-

[8] Bismarck became Chancellor of Germany in 1862 and for twenty-eight years thereafter stood out not merely as the most imposing figure in Germany but as one of the most important personalities in Europe. He was typical of the Junker class from which he sprang in his contempt for democratic institutions and liberal principles generally. An intrigant of the first order, he consolidated the German states into an Empire under Prussian domination. The Socialists hated him because they hated his militarism and the ruthless autocratic qualities of his statecraft. He in turn hated them because in his estimation the spread of socialist ideals among the working classes was a threat to law and order and the stability of the Empire which he had created.

spiracy of events finally delivered the Party completely into his hands. In 1878 two unsuccessful attempts were made on the life of the aging Emperor William I. Here at last was a pretext and it was immediately seized upon. Both deeds were promptly laid at the door of the socialists, and their suppression was demanded. In the excitement and indignation of the moment Bismarck was completely successful. The Social Democratic Party was outlawed and all of its activities were rigorously suppressed.

Since the socialist unions as yet had scarcely discovered either mentally or physically an identity distinct from that of the socialist movement to which they owed their existence, disaster to this movement meant disaster to its trade union offspring, still nourished within its own body. Certainly as between the two, political socialism and economic trade unionism, German police could scarcely be relied upon to make distinctions of which the workers themselves had only faint glimmerings of an approaching awareness. And so in this period of fear and uncertainty as to what might be construed to be pure and simple trade unionism and thus within the law and what tainted with political socialism and therefore illegitimate, the safest and most popular procedure was to forego all group activity whatsoever. The immediate result of the anti-socialist legislation, therefore, was the virtual disappearance not only of socialist activity but of the Free or socialist trade unions as well.

Movements filled with youthful vitality, however, and as thoroughly in accord with their environment as the trade union in a rapidly expanding industrial society could scarcely be expected to succumb permanently to a single legislative obstacle. Consequently, under the stimulating influence of returning prosperity in the decade of the eighties there were signs of revival, cautious and experimental at first but growing in assurance as the wave of reactionism, of which the anti-socialist laws were merely a symptom, began to recede.

Of obvious urgency to the trade unions under existing conditions was the necessity of clearing themselves of all suspicion of subservience to the outlawed Social Democratic Party and of demonstrating that they stood on their own feet. Thus the reappearance of labor organizations in various innocuous guises was signalized by a resounding lip-service to the political *status quo* and, simultaneously, a careful weeding from positions of leadership in the unions of all those who were likewise prominent in the affairs of the Party.

It was not so much from the anti-socialist laws, however, that the unions were to be placed in jeopardy as from the general spirit of reactionary intolerance of which these laws were the most conspicuous symptom. The reaction from the Revolution of 1848 had brought with it throughout the original German states, and thereby bequeathed to Germany, legislation for the general suppression of every type of political association. The law in Prussia was that, while societies of a political nature might exist locally, the association of these locals in any fashion would automatically make them illegal and subject to dissolution.

Such legislation in the light of the social progress since the time of its enactment was an obvious anachronism, and the difficulty of the position in which it placed labor organizations, now that it was re-invoked, is all too apparent. Any labor organization attempting to promote or influence the character of legislation for its own protection, or indeed legislation of any kind and for any purpose, might on that account be adjudged a political association. In Prussia, even correspondence between locals of this "political" nature might in turn constitute political combination and as such be illegal, rendering the offending organizations subject to dissolution and their officials to fines or jail sentences. It was not until 1892, two years, be it noted, after the anti-socialist laws were repealed, that prosecutions under these old acts ceased to be made.

While this circumstance did not destroy the trade union movement, needless to say it left a lasting impression on the nature of its development. Of particular importance in the face of such legislation was the necessity of distinguishing between economic and political activity and of demonstrating that distinction. In groping for some such line of cleavage labor inadvertently found its way toward a slightly different concept of a much more permanent importance; namely, that, even though the trade unions were both in and of the socialist movement, the two were in no sense completely identical and, furthermore, that the ends pursued by each might not only be different, they might often be actually at variance with each other.

Out of this process of enforced self-analysis looking toward the discovery of its own mind and its own purpose, came the crystallization of two opposing groups within the trade union movement itself, known respectively as the localists and the centrists.

While superficially, as the names imply, the point at issue between these opposing factions was concerning the relative desirability of purely local and autonomous organizations in contrast to the centralization of these locals nationally into their respective trade groups, the difference was actually more fundamental and involved a conflict in basic philosophies. A contemplation of the legislation concerning political association makes perfectly clear that sentiment for integration, the aim of the centrists, meant sentiment in favor of surrendering all pretense at existing as a political body and the limitation of attention to what might be interpreted as purely economic functions. By that same token the localists by their stand served notice that in their estimation labor's battle was to be fought primarily on the political front and that the centrists' retreat from that front and their tacit acceptance thereby of the political *status quo* was a betrayal of the best interests of the working class as a whole.

That the revolutionary orthodoxy of the mass of workers was beginning to waver in the face of the growing appeal of economic expedience now became quite evident, for in spite of the active aid of influential Party members, who naturally sympathized with the localist point of view, the localist cause was hopelessly lost. At Germany's first General Trade Union Congress, held in Halberstadt in 1892, only 10,000 localists were represented in contrast to the 350,000 who voted to make the national union the basis of future organization. Disgruntled, disappointed, but inflexible, the localists withdrew from the conference. Never able to enlist a membership large enough to make themselves really significant, they finally, in 1907, allied themselves with Germany's struggling syndicalist movement.

By this conflict the unions achieved clearly a shift to the right and solidified their conservative strength. For not only had this event called for a clarification of issues and a careful weighing of advantages; by inducing the secession of the localists it had purged unionism of its most vigorous political and revolutionary influence.

Since 1890 saw the repeal of the anti-socialist legislation and 1892 the end of the application of the laws against political association, the labor movement, whether on the economic or the political front, was now free to pursue its own ends without serious interference. Although external difficulties were thus seemingly disposed of, events began to move rapidly toward the crystallization of a new problem which the localist-centrist controversy had already foreshadowed. Since it was growing increasingly obvious that the interests of union and Party were not always served in the same fashion, that problem was as to the nature of the ultimate relationship between the two organizations. Socialism in the past had called trade unionism into being to serve its own political and revolutionary ends. Must unions now, in consequence, exist as an agency merely of Party glorification and under Party control? Must they continue indefinitely to submerge their own interests if necessary and to sacrifice the day-by-day advantage of the workers on the altar of abstraction and Party doctrine? The answer, at least for the moment, was to lie largely in the degree of success of the trade union movement and in the consequent growth of its own sense of importance and self-reliance.

Abstractly at least, the Free unions had been very successful. Even during the years of legal oppression they had made progress and at the first General Trade Union Congress (1892) were able to show a membership of approximately 350,000, a figure which gains some added significance when compared to the corresponding 66,000 members of the Hirsch-Dunckers, whose unionizing program had escaped all legal interference.

The success of the unions, however, pales considerably when compared with the success of the Party. The latter's demonstrated powers of resistance to Bismarck's efforts to destroy it bore testimony to the prophetic ability of the radical leader Richter, who opposed such legislation, saying that Social Democracy was more to be feared with the legislation than without it. Such proved to be the case. Pervading the whole socialist structure at this stage of its development was that emotional fervor which accompanies the founding of new religions. Persecution came, thus, not as a destroyer so much as a mighty stimulant. It embittered and hardened the resolution of Party members and clothed the whole cause with a sanctity which otherwise it might not have possessed. Accordingly, when the ban was lifted in 1890, there appeared to mock its erstwhile destroyers not the Party of 1881 with its 312,-000 members but, in its stead, one with a membership of 1,427,000, able to send thirty-five of its members to seats in the Reichstag and rightfully to pose as the strongest single political force in the Empire.

In the face of such circumstances it is not strange that Party leaders should have suffered from profound illusions concerning the imminence of their complete triumph and should have acted accordingly.

In this new sense of importance the unions were not able wholly to share. They occupied now a rather curious position. Inasmuch as they had been created for one single purpose; namely, to glorify the Party and to help insure its revolutionary triumph, the nearer the approach of that triumph the nearer, also, the time when from a doctrinal point of view the real significance of the unions would be ended. Thus the old Lassallean indifference to such institutions now came again to pervade the whole socialist group. Even Bebel and Liebknecht, to whom most of all the unions owed their existence, at the Party convention in 1893 agreed in insisting that too much must not be expected of trade unionism, for, as Liebknecht had previously expressed it, "Before the trade unions will have a chance the banners of socialism will already have been waving over the citadels of capitalism."[9] Thus the very success of the Party, in its own eyes at least, deprived the unions of the major part of their reason for existence.

[9] Perlman, *op. cit.*, p. 78.

General Trade Union Congress and the Events Leading to the Declaration of Union Autonomy

In the meantime, however, the unions, although still composed primarily of Party members holding fast to the socialist faith, were beginning to find their own justification for living and to move, although with a great show of reluctance, within the orbit of their own specific interests.

Employers themselves made a solid contribution toward this new type of cohesion. In 1890, having organized themselves into an association for the purpose of combatting the threatened expansion of trade unionism, they decided to make a display of their strength by declaring a general lockout against all those who had participated in the May Day celebrations which had just been observed in Germany for the first time. Inasmuch as the renunciation of the union was to be the only basis of reinstatement, the unions, now that the anti-socialist and anti-combination laws were behind them, seemed suddenly faced with the necessity of fighting for their lives all over again.

Happily for them the will to survive and hence to fight had not been dimmed by their recent experiences. Reaction was prompt and vigorous. Recognizing the essential impotence, in the face of this new situation, of the scattering and localized efforts that had characterized German workers' organizations heretofore, they resolved to meet integration with integration, and before the end of the year a conference of trade union presidents had been held in Berlin for the purpose of bringing this condition about. This conference had as its significant fruition Germany's first General Trade Union Congress, which convened at Halberstadt in 1892. With this Congress the modern trade union movement of Germany had its beginning.

The scheme of organization contrived here was in its essentials not unlike that of the American Federation of Labor. Structurally the German organization was to consist of a federation of national unions organized under the executive headship of a "General Commission" of (originally) seven members to be chosen by the General Trade Union Congress at its regular recurring sessions. Functionally the primary purpose of this federation was the dissemination of propaganda in favor of trade unionism, the publication of a trade union journal, the *Correspondenzblatt*, and the collection and publication of labor statistics.

Plagued still by that conflict concerning method and purpose which had struggled for dominance in the minds of union members since the beginning of the union movement, the first years of this organization were halting and uncertain. Nevertheless the general structural plan remained practically unchanged, and within its broad framework as originally conceived German trade unionism was able to achieve its subsequent greatness.

It is significant now to observe that, important as this step was as a means toward an effective trade unionism, it was made in the face of strong opposition from the Party. The cause of this opposition is quite apparent. In the first place, by this solidification the trade unions obviously achieved a vastly greater industrial significance. But from the socialist point of view that very achievement was portentous of evil, becoming a snare and a delusion if, as well it might, it should help induce unionists to forget their historic function as revolutionists and to succumb to the appeal of their immediate but relatively trifling successes as trade unionists. In the second place, Party leaders were jealous for the continuation of their undisputed supremacy in the working-class movement and could scarcely contemplate with equanimity the appearance of a possible counter-authority within their own dominion. The German proletariat, so far as they were concerned, could serve but one master, and that must be the Social Democratic Party.

The history of German trade unionism from now on is increasingly a demonstration that between the social philosophy of the trade unionist and that of the socialist intellectual there is a fundamental difference; and that, regardless of the conspiracy of circumstances by which that difference can be kept concealed or submerged, eventually it comes to the top and makes itself felt.

Of the various issues which led to the crystallization of a distinctly trade union point of view and to the realization on the part of trade unionists that their attitude was inherently irreconcilable with that of the fostering Party, four, at least, are worthy of mention. They are: the problem of trade union benefits for the unemployed, the use of the collective agreement, the observance of May Day, and the use of the general strike.

In considering first the problem of trade union benefits, it is necessary at once to observe that Bismarck in his attempts to neutralize the appeal of the rising socialist movement and to win German workers away from its influence had, incidentally as it were, achieved for Germany the distinction of being one of the great pioneers in the field of social insurance. Indeed the only significant industrial hazard against which workers now lacked protection was that of unemployment. In the face of this fact the question with which the German unions were wrestling was that of the desirability of following the example of their English colleagues and of building up out-of-work benefit schemes of their own.

From the distinctly unionist point of view the rationality of such a procedure was scarcely open to question. By such devices the union is at once made for the worker a source of refuge from which he tends no longer lightly to cut himself off. Discipline is thus strengthened and added stability is achieved. This, especially in the formative days, is very important. Unemployment benefits, moreover, as is well known, have the particular merit of minimizing the pressure of unemployment and of lessening the probability that men in times of labor trouble may betray the union and become strike breakers or be forced to violate standard union practices.

In spite of the clearness of the case the sentiment in favor of such benefits spread slowly, compelled as it was to make headway against strong socialist opposition both within and outside of the trade unions. Why, it was reasoned, should the workers by their contributions bear the whole burden of a calamity which not they but a capitalistic system had produced? Besides, the very success of such a venture might prove a misfortune. For to the degree that the impact of unemployment was lessened, to that same degree would the workers be inclined to waver in their resolution to blot out in due time that economic system which was the ultimate source of this evil. However, it was the trade union point of view which finally prevailed. The second General Trade Union Congress (1895) gave to the idea its official endorsement, and from that time on it was urged upon all union organizations.

The second issue mentioned was the use of the collective agreement. This became a basis for controversy particularly after the signing of such an agreement by the printers in 1896. From the revolutionary point of view such an institution is naturally unacceptable. It represents not so much a proletarian triumph, in which the bourgeois employer is forced to surrender his traditional and jealously defended right to run his own business as he sees fit; it represents, rather, on labor's part an acquiescence in the existing order and the shameful abandonment of that most sacred principle, the class struggle. The self-help idea, furthermore, which collective bargaining involves, obviously represents a wide departure from what in Germany seemed to be a normal tendency; namely, an inclination to look to the state for help and to concentrate on the political front. Nevertheless at the General Trade Union Congress of 1899 the collective agreement was stamped with official approval, and its use from then on was encouraged.

A third basis of dissension, that of the observance of May Day, was precipitated by the Second Socialist International in 1889, when it designated May first as a labor holiday to be observed throughout the proletarian world in some appropriate fashion. While this in no way involved socialists and trade unionists in doctrinal differences, it did focus attention on distinctly contradictory conceptions of social expedience. For since its birth this holiday had met the uniform and determined resistance of employers, and its observance by workers had been always at the risk of lockouts or wholesale dismissals. The union dilemma under these conditions is quite apparent. If the holiday were observed and dismissals followed, the Party was indeed glorified, but it was up to the union to come to the support of its now unemployed members. If, on the other hand, in the interests of security there was a disposition not to participate in the celebration, those workers or organizations which failed to respond were open to the taunt of being cowardly deserters from the great battle which was being waged for their own ultimate well-being. From the trade union point of view, tending as it now did to emphasize the practical and the immediate, service to Party was so obviously in this instance disservice to self that mounting dissatisfaction and internal stresses became inevitable. This dissatisfaction in no small degree contributed to the climactic break in 1905.

The difficulty which precipitated the final rupture between unions and Party was the problem of the use of the general strike. Following a resolution by the International Labor Congress at Amsterdam in 1904, favoring its adoption as an instrument of last resort in class warfare, it immediately became one of the leading issues before the succeeding trade union congress and also before the Party convention.

For the unions this was a matter of major importance. The last few years had been for them years of very successful expansion and increasing significance, and to underwrite now a scheme as revolutionary as that of the general strike seemed an unwarranted and profitless flirtation with disaster. If due to their indulgence in this radical gesture the government, led by fear or impatience, should reinvoke the repressive legislation from which they had so recently escaped, most of the gains since that escape would be lost.

It was quite apparent, also, that between the Party and the unions the risk was an unequal one. The former, outlawed and driven underground, as has just been demonstrated, could not only survive; it could flourish. Unions, on the other hand, must work in the open, and outlawry would unquestionably have meant their destruction. It is not surprising, consequently, that the general strike was rejected by the unions with uncompromising vigor.

This act excited at once the resentment of Party leaders, who charged the unions with an arrogant usurpation of authority, inasmuch as they had presumed to dictate to their members how they should react to a political question, a field of activity, it was assumed, which fell wholly and solely within the natural jurisdiction of the Party. To make the situation even more difficult, the Party at its convention then proceeded, in effect at least, to accept the Amsterdam recommendation and to vote for the general strike.

Here at last was the impasse toward which events had long been tending—unions and Party each publicly pledged to a diametrically opposing position on an issue of major importance. In this crisis it was the socialists who made the most conspicuous gesture of climbing down from their position. But in spite of the conciliatory efforts of Party leaders, particularly Bebel, the unions remained obdurate. Now under the inspiring leadership of Legien they stubbornly refused to recede by one jot from their original determination to concede nothing of priority to the Party when the union or its principles might be considered to be endangered. The child had obviously outgrown parental authority, and wisely the parent accepted the situation as cheerfully as possible. Since the relative size and prestige of the two groups had altered considerably since 1890 (the Free unions now had 1,345,000 members), any other course by endangering a complete alienation of the trade unionists would have been foolishly shortsighted. Accordingly an arrangement was concluded by which the Party agreed to yield completely its claim to authority over the trade unions and to coöperate with the Federation and its General Commission rather than to seek to control it. This arrangement, ratified by the Party convention the next year (1906), became the celebrated Mannheim Agreement.

Relationship between Party and Unions after Mannheim; Revisionism

It must not be assumed that with this declaration of independence and the recognition of trade union autonomy there came about, as time passed, an increasing divergence between the union and the Party point of view or that there was a growing lack of sympathy between the two organizations. For, quite to the contrary, this clarification of limits of authority and nature of function had a wholesome pacifying influence on both groups. "After Mannheim," as Professor Perlman expresses it, "harmony reigned."

While union membership was no longer held as a prerequisite to membership in the Party, nevertheless the Party was still largely made up of members of trade unions, and, conversely, unionists were for the most part still allied to the Party. Furthermore the very interesting fact is that the unions in deciding to try to fit their program into a world of tangible realities rather than into a world of philosophical concepts were merely taking a direction in which, as we shall now see, the Party itself was turning and was destined soon openly to follow.

So long as the socialists had been all aglow with their impressive triumph over Bismarck's schemes for their extermination and were waiting breathlessly for the breakdown of the existing order, orthodoxy was easy and unity prevailed. Even those variations in the conception of tactics which were the natural product of the extremity of their situation during the period of anti-socialist legislation now melted away, and the platform adopted at Erfurt in 1891, as they prepared once more to live openly, represented a rededication to a creed so thoroughly Marxian as to seem in part like a restatement of the Communist Manifesto.

Victory, however, did not continue to be added to victory with the ease and rapidity that past experience seemed to promise. The conviction so confidently expressed by Bebel at the Erfurt convention that "bourgeois society is working so mightily towards its own downfall that we need only to wait for the moment when we shall have to take up the power falling from its hands . . . there are few in this hall who will not live to see the day" began more and more to have the air of a wishful prophecy rather than that of a tangible fact.

While the voting strength of the Party did indeed continue to increase with gratifying rapidity and parliamentary representation at a corresponding pace, these gains brought no practical political advantage. The increasing demonstration of power on the part of the socialists had brought with it an increasing tendency to coalition on the part of the opposition; so that in spite of seeming progress the ultimate goal—socialist domination—remained as distant as ever. Furthermore the fall of profits, the increase of misery, the intensification of crises, the sharpening of the class struggle—in short the whole Marxian category of fatal diseases undermining, presumably, the capitalist order—as time passed showed no alarming tendency either to appear or to increase in their intensity. On the contrary the phenomenal expansion of German industry which now began to get under way brought with it a perversely increasing prosperity, which seemed, for the time being at least, to belie the whole doleful socialist prophecy and to drive the expected social revolution farther and farther into the realms of speculation and unreality.

The logic of this trend of events was inescapable. Evidently the capitalistic system was endowed with a vitality which Marx in the wishfulness of his thinking had never been willing to grant it. The kingdom of heaven was not yet at hand.

This fact, borne in upon the minds of Party leaders, seemed now to necessitate a reappraisal of tactics. The original attitude of "mere inactive waiting," which conforms so perfectly with the fatalistic qualities of Marxism and the general illusion of socialism's imminence, now began to appear much less satisfactory. Moreover, while the spectacular successes of Social Democracy had drawn into its ranks a mass of mere camp-followers, mercenaries, and malcontents of all kinds, it was perfectly clear that as a party it was still a proletarian institution and that whatever endangered the loyalty or confidence of its working-class members endangered likewise its very existence as well. Since it is recognized that workers are essentially realists with a keen sense of "time preference," obviously it would grow increasingly difficult either to placate or inspire them with checks on the bank of the coming socialist state as that state faded farther and farther into the future. Thus Social Democracy, it began to appear, was more and more to be called upon to forsake the future and to justify itself to its constituents in terms of the affairs of the moment.

It is not to be supposed, of course, that there was complete unanimity in the socialist reaction to this situation. Theories tend always to a hardy existence and to survive the conditions which justified their birth. Then, too, Marxism was a religion, and the most conclusive evidence penetrates with difficulty minds already fortified by contrary emotions. Thus the Party found itself once again divided into two factions. One was determined to observe to the utmost the letter of the original Marxian revelation, particularly as it was interpreted in the Erfurt program; the other, convinced that faith in dogma must give way to some very solid works in behalf of labor now struggling to cope with the conditions immediately surrounding it, argued for a more realistic program.

This latter, the Revisionist point of view, found in Eduard Bernstein a very able exponent. Under the mellowing influence of long association with the English Fabians during his years of exile in London Bernstein's original Marxian orthodoxy had yielded perceptibly. The point of view to which he and his fellow Revisionists now adhered was that in view of the Marxian error concerning the speed of social evolution it became necessary for the Social Democratic Party to devote itself more to the problems of reform and less to those of revolution. To do this it must forsake its old pose of abstraction and cynical aloofness, as in fancy it witnessed the existing bourgeois society moving head on to its inevitable destruction, and must devote every effort to the determination of the policy of the existing state where that policy affected the day-by-day problems of proletarian welfare.

This controversy, which had been smoldering for years, particularly in the more democratic South Germany, was actively precipitated by Bernstein's letter to the Congress of the Party at Stuttgart in 1898 and came to a climax in the Congress at Dresden in 1903. At this latter meeting Revisionism was defeated by an overwhelming vote, and thus, officially at least, the Party washed its hands, presumably for all time, of all responsibility for interfering with immediate social issues in the interests of reform.

This repudiation, however, may be interpreted as more in the nature of a refusal to publicly acknowledge and sanction a shift in Party attitude than as a denial of all interest in current reforms or in the means of their achievement. Little by little within the Party the demands of orthodoxy were yielding steadily before the demands of expedience. So, while the creed, indeed, remained the same, devotion to it was being noticeably altered.

This change, occurring as it did gradually, almost imperceptibly, was hastened by some events of particular significance. One of these, surely, was the necessity itself for the acknowledgment of trade union independence at Mannheim. There, perhaps for the first time, Party members were shocked out of their complacency concerning the "manifest destiny" of the socialist movement in

Germany and the comfortable conviction that the very stars in their courses fought to bring them victory.

Close upon the heels of Mannheim came the so-called "Hottentot" election of 1907. The issue was the Kaiser's program of imperialism and colonial expansion. Nothing, it is obvious, could represent much more completely a flouting of the socialist point of view. Accordingly the Party girt itself to lead the opposition. In this election, fought as it was in an atmosphere of emotionalism and in the face of a rising tide of nationalist and pan-Germanic sentiment, the socialists found themselves supporting a hopelessly unpopular issue and were swept back with the loss of almost half of their seats in the Reichstag. This reverse had a tremendously sobering effect and brought in its wake a marked softening in the tone of the internationalist and anti-militaristic utterances of Party members.

The coming of the World War, however, was the climactic event contributing to this steady "degeneration." With its outbreak almost the last vestige of the old revolutionary philosophy of the seventies vanished. Internationalism and loyalty to class were swallowed up in a surging loyalty to country. In spite of previous stout utterances and some internal dissensions, in its historic "fourth of August" decision the Social Democratic Party voted solidly for war credits, and thenceforth, instead of posing as an enemy of the existing "class" state, waiting only for a favorable opportunity for its destruction, it became that state's strong and open supporter, asking in return only some modifications in the interests of democracy and social reform.

With this return of German workers, first the trade unionists and now their intellectual sponsors and leaders, from the realms of the abstract and the speculative to a world of realities, where human welfare is demonstrably, at least in part, a matter of one's own achievement, there is added another impressive increment to the mass of evidence that workers are not social philosophers. Neither are they an "abstract mass" willing to face years of misery for which there is a possible alternative in order that some prophecy of ultimate historic destiny may be fulfilled.

Because of this abandonment by the Social Democratic Party of its historic revolutionary point of view and its corresponding change of front the line of demarcation between German socialism and German trade unionism once again sank into obscurity. Fundamentally their attitudes toward the existing order were now identical; neither demanded its destruction; both sought its reform. The difference became thus primarily one of choice of technique. In this respect old distinctions persisted, for, while the socialists strove along the political front, the trade unionists still placed their faith in a more direct economic action.

So far as prestige was concerned, this shift in relationships favored the unions. Since both groups were now opportunistic, relative advantage lay with whichever one demonstrably was most likely to "bring home the bacon." In this respect the trade union program with its greater objectivity and precision was able to present the more effective appeal.

Before going farther with the discussion of the Free unions and their socialist relationships it seems appropriate at this point to introduce the discussion of the Christian unions, the last of the three important types of organizations to be founded.

The Christian Unions

The Christian unions, now international in scope, had their beginning in Germany in the decade of the 1880's under the fostering influence of the local priesthood of the Roman Catholic Church. They were born of a conviction of the need for some type of workers' organization and, at the same time, of a fear of the demoralizing influence of the Free unions with their strongly socialist and anti-religious tendencies. This movement, disorganized and groping at first, was integrated and given direction by the papal encyclical *Rerum Novarum* in 1891.

Because of the sectarian character of their origin the area of influence of these unions and their possibilities for growth were considerably limited. While 18 national trade unions, covering an equal number of occupations, were included, the bulk of the membership occurred among the miners, metal workers, textile workers of the strongly Catholic Rhine Provinces and Westphalia, and in agriculture. Numbering approximately 1,049,000 at the height of their career (1922), they were obviously much more successful than the Hirsch-Dunckers but far short of the achievements of the Free unions.

While they showed a general tendency to emphasize the significance of the individual, there was no inclination to accept as a necessary corollary that doctrine of economic liberalism which in a competitive society makes possible the exploitation of the many for the benefit of the few. On the other hand, while admitting the tendency toward the occurrence of economic classes and class interests, they denied the socialist conception of the class struggle. In conformity with this attitude they maintained that the need for organization was not that of a more effective promotion of conflict with employers but rather a more effective settlement of disputes with these employers in accordance with the ideals of the Christian religion. It is to be expected, then, that the methods of the Christian unions had a tendency to be less militant than those of their socialist contemporaries, great reliance being placed on the possibilities of economic reform through labor-capital coöperation to increase production and through peaceful negotiation. The trade agreement, in their estimation, should be supported by industrial courts and shop committees for the adjudication and adjustment of grievances. Great emphasis was also placed on the building up of a strong union treasury, not, as in the instance of the more militant unions, to be used as a war chest in time of trouble but to serve, rather, as a basis for inclusive benefit programs. The strike, as implied, was considered a weapon of last resort, to be used only under the most extreme provocation.

While in some countries these unions in keeping with their origin are strictly Catholic, representing an arm of the Church and functioning under its guidance, in Germany, nominally at least, they were inter-denominational. Due to this mixed membership (although to the end they remained very distinctly sectarian) and to the necessity of making many collective agreements with Protestant employers it seemed expedient to sever direct and official connection with the Church and its control. The more important liaison was rather with the political Catholic Center Party. Here the relationship was quite similar to that existing between the Free unions and the Social Democratic Party. One significant point of difference in these relationships, however, lay in the fact that the Free unions adhered to a body more revolutionary than themselves, while the Christian unions, on the other hand, adhered to an essentially capitalistic or middle-class institution from which they could expect little coöperation if they undertook too vigorous a program. The conservatism of this political alliance of the Christian unions naturally added to the suspicion and distrust with which they were viewed by their more radical and more numerous contemporaries, the Free unions.

While it is true that in the industries in which they

existed simultaneously the Christian and Free unions cooperated at times in making collective agreements and in strictly economic affairs, the relationship between the two was far from friendly. To the Christian unions the Free unions were socialistic and wholly worldly in their approach to their problems, and their expansion, consequently, was to be considered in the light of a social menace. To the Free Unions, on the other hand, the Christian unions were without excuse for being, organizations whose very existence was a betrayal of the working class as a whole. Too small to be of much assistance, they were, nevertheless, sufficiently large in certain districts to hamper seriously by their passive inclinations the more vigorous course of action which the Free unions wished to pursue.

The original bitterness between these two groups was softened somewhat, as time passed, by inevitable changes in the character of both. The Free unions, as already demonstrated, grew less and less Marxian and "ultimate" and more and more an agency for the direct relief of the working class by whatever means seemed to be available. The same forces which compelled them to this less doctrinaire position compelled the Christian unions, likewise, to one less idealistic and passive. Labor, regardless of creed or religious conviction, as has often been contended, demands results and will not over a long period of time accept the domination of any organization which does not obtain them.

Driven together in this fashion, these two organizations before the time of Nazi liquidation had achieved an attitude of mutual courtesy, if not one of complete accord.

Labor's Mounting Prestige during the War and in the Post-War Period

Concerning the general aspects of the more modern phase of Germany's working-class movement one may say that the first World War found it already arrived at a high degree of intellectual maturity. The changes of the War and post-War period represent, therefore, not so much significant changes in points of view as fluctuations in the power and prestige of these organizations, whose social philosophy had already been well established.

While organized labor had survived the reactionary efforts of Bismarck aimed at its outlawry and destruction, it must not be assumed that from that time on it enjoyed either popular or political favor. The situation was quite the reverse. Throughout the pre-War period the Free unions continued to suffer socially from the stigma of their identification with the "godless and faithless" and unpatriotic Social Democratic Party. Politically, in addition, the whole organized labor movement found itself falling heir to the enmity of the young Emperor William II. Stung by labor's unresponsiveness to his early and rather ostentatious attempts at its wooing, he turned in his irritation to a program of repression which was extraordinarily severe. Throughout the remainder of his reign he consistently represented the union as an institution to which no loyal German could belong and as a thing which should be hampered and suppressed wherever opportunity afforded.

The unanimous decision of the Social Democratic Party to support the War and to sustain the existing government together with the declaration of an industrial truce by union organizations, which placed themselves wholly at the state's disposal, brought an immediate reversal in popular feeling. It was with the Revolution following the War and the formation of the Republic, however, that workers as union members really came to their own, winning their way to general esteem as a responsive and responsible social force. This they accomplished by helping the nation to survive those troublous days without the collapse of the existing economic regime, a regime which they themselves had helped to build up and in which, Marx notwithstanding, they had much more at stake than their chains. They recognized clearly its intricate character and the danger of laying violent or ignorant hands on its delicate framework. Under these circumstances they became its resolute and efficient defenders, protecting it from the rising tide of communist influence on the left, while, at the same time, by their general strike they forestalled the Kapp Putsch from the right. Thus with the Weimar Constitution and the Republic it came about quite naturally that organized labor, an institution long outcast and rejected, enjoyed for a time considerable social esteem.

So far as sheer numerical strength was concerned, the War and post-War period brought wide fluctuations whose net result was strongly upward. In its immediate effect, of course, the War brought a great decline, since many trade union members were enrolled in the army. The membership of the Free unions sank from two and a half millions at its outbreak to about a million in 1915. With the end of hostilities, however, and the return of the soldiers to their peace-time occupations all unions found themselves suddenly expanded to almost embarrassing proportions. In 1923 the peak was reached with a total union membership of more than thirteen millions.

Since a considerable part of this influx represented people who had no real conception of trade unionism but who hoped merely to use the union as a convenient means to a more rapid economic rehabilitation, a certain amount of disillusionment and dissatisfaction on their part was inevitable. Unemployment and the rapid depreciation in the value of the mark added to the union problem and to the general restlessness. Masses began forsaking the unions with the same precipitation with which they had

GERMANY 191

joined them and in so doing tended to become the raw material of a rising communist threat.

In spite of these losses, however, the unions at the close of the Republic were still able to boast of a numerical strength far in excess of that of the pre-War period. In 1931 the distribution of membership among the three central organizations was as follows: Free unions 4,418,000, Hirsch-Duncker unions 181,000, Christian unions 578,000.

DUALISM ONCE AGAIN

It could not be assumed, of course, that the integrity of the union movement itself could wholly escape the demoralizing and disintegrating influence of German defeat and of the disappearance of the old political order. Under these conditions the plague of all organized effort, dualism or secession, was bound to spring up again and to grow acute.

Affecting particularly the Free unions was the split which occurred in the Social Democratic Party while the War was still in progress. To many Party members it had become increasingly clear, as time passed, that the War was not, as they had been led to believe in 1914, a purely defensive affair. As a result, that appearance of unanimity with which they had blessed it and pledged support to the existing state was becoming ever more difficult to maintain. Finally in 1917 the breach came, and a minority group of the more radical members broke away to form the Independent Socialist Party. By this gesture, after more than forty years of unified effort socialism was once again divided into two opposing factions.

Since union members still, with little exception, were involved in Party membership also, this break threatened to place the socialist unions once again in the precise position from which they had escaped with the amalgamation of the Marxian and Lassallean branches at Gotha years before.

In the face of this situation the succeeding trade union congress in an attempt to neutralize this threat declared for the complete political neutrality of the trade union movement. In so doing, it will be noticed, labor shifted farther still from its original position and toward the pure and simple concept of trade union function. In sympathy, however, the old entente between the Social Democratic Party and the Free unions remained essentially intact. The Independent Socialists had little success in their attempts to win trade unionists to a more radical position.

The same conditions which rendered organized labor relatively unresponsive to the Independent Socialists gave it a high degree of immunity, also, to the efforts of the communists either to bring about its overthrow or to lure it in a more radical direction. The lack of cohesion which crept into the unions following the war on account of the influx of fair-weather unionists, soldiers, workers' soviets, etc., together with the fall in real wages due to inflation and widespread unemployment, made the situation of the established unions for a time seemingly precarious. A spirit of unrest pervaded the country, and there was a growing tendency toward unauthorized strikes and for union control to be disregarded. The communists were quick to take advantage of this state of affairs in the hope of destroying the existing "bourgeois" unions and replacing them with a single proletarian organization whose purpose should be the conquest of political power. All attempts at boring both from within and without, however, proved of no avail. The conservative union majority held the situation firmly within its grasp.

A more serious threat to the continued dominance of a now thoroughly conservative trade unionism was the rise of the works councils. These institutions, which were as old as the trade union movement itself in Germany, had existed as an essentially conservative influence, wholly acceptable to the Christian and Hirsch-Duncker unions and meeting the qualified approval of the Free unions as well. During the War, as already indicated, a strong left wing movement had grown up among the workers, within which the Russian revolutionary phrase "all power to the soviets" had become quite familiar and appealing. With the German Revolution the surging popularity of this idea and the multiplication of soldiers' and workers' councils suddenly transformed the innocuous works councils, whose worst offense heretofore, at least in the eyes of the Free unions, had been their tendency toward class collaboration, into a potential revolutionary agency of great significance.

To masses of German proletarians now revelling in a new sense of social importance and self-sufficiency, existing trade unionism with its bureaucracy, its purely reformist character, and its identification with the old regime was something of an anachronism. It was the hope of the left wing of the socialist unions, as well as that of the communists, to use the councils as focal points for the crystallization of a dual and revolutionary labor movement, which would seize the leadership formerly enjoyed by conservative trade unions and force them into the background.

The unions, however, were not caught without a will to survive nor a capacity for self-defense. Realizing that the idea of the works councils or soviets had taken deep root among the workers, they wisely chose not to attempt to crush but rather to control it. This acquiescence was signalized not only by their collaboration in and acceptance of the Works Council Act of 1920, which established these institutions, but also by their participation in the framing of the Weimar Constitution, which anticipated the Act. Much was done in both instances to help insure the continuation of union ascendency and works council subservience.

At the first general congress of works councils in Germany, held in Berlin in October, 1920, the relationship which the councils were to maintain toward the trade union was formally determined. The vote was a demonstration of the advantage of "machine" methods, to which the unions were able to have recourse. The organized effort of those who sought to place the works councils under the control of the trade unions overwhelmed the disorganized enthusiasm of those who opposed it. By a decisive vote the representatives of the councils expressed their determination to become an integral part of the trade union movement and to accept the plan of integration which had been prepared by the trade union leaders.

While officially this vote ended the serious threats to trade union supremacy, the actual situation, as the communist activity would indicate, did not involve that degree of finality. Leftist defeat, naturally, did not eliminate leftist sentiment, and the enduring dissensions between unions and councils continued to the end of the Republic.

INDEX

Allan, W., 39
Allemanists, 88-89; and the bourses, 97
Amalgamated Society of Carpenters, 39
Amalgamated Society of Engineers, 37-39
American Federation of Labor, 2, 9, 33, 34; compared to the British Trades Union Congress, 11-13, 14; compared to the New Model, 50-52; compared to the German General Trade Union Congress, 174
Anarchism, and syndicalism, 106-107, 109-110
Anarchists, 87, 89; and the C. G. T. U., 136
Applegarth, Robert, 39

Bakunin, Michael, and the general strike, 113; imprint on syndicalism, 87, 109
Barberet, J., 84, 85
Barberetists, 85, 86-87
Bebel, August, and the Free unions, 162-163, 164-165; on trade unionism, 172; on the downfall of bourgeois society, 180-181; mentioned, 179
Becker, Bernhard, 158
Benefit programs, importance of in British unions, 35, 37, 38; as an issue in German unions, 175-176
Bernstein, Eduard, 182-183
Bismarck, Chancellor, 166 n; attacks Social Democratic Party, 166-167; and social insurance, 175; mentioned, 162, 180, 189
"Black Friday," 68
Blanc, Louis, 81
Blanquists, 83, 89

Bourse du travail, 95-98
Briand, Aristide, 112, 113
Brousse, Paul, 87
Broussists, 88-89
Buchez, P., 81
Burns, John, quoted, 44; mentioned, 45, 48

Capitalism, Marxian conception of, 3-5
Centrists, 169-170
Cercle de l'Union Ouvrière, formed, 84; mentioned, 92
Charter of Amiens, resolutions, 104-105; and post-War disputes, 134-135; mentioned, 75, 85, 124, 126, 133
Chartism, 30-32; mentioned, 27
Christian unions, British, 72; French, 76; German, 148, 185-188
Citrine, Sir Walter, 19
Class consciousness, as a factor in the British labor movement, 10
Coal miners (British), 66-68
Collective agreement, and the C. G. T., 129; as an issue in German unions, 175, 176-177
Combination, laws affecting the right of, British: Trade Union Act, 41; Criminal Law Amendment Act, 41; Conspiracy and Protection of Property Act, 42; Trade Disputes and Trade Unions Act, 72; French: Le Chapelier, 77, 80; proclamation of tolérance, 82, 90; law of 1884, 90, 91, 95, 111, 133; German: General Prussian Code, 149; Industrial Code, 149; repeal of laws against, 150. See also Combination Acts

[195]

INDEX

Combination Acts, 18-20, 25, 26, 27
Commune (Paris), effect of on French labor, 82-83; on German, 166
Communism, influence of on British labor, 73-74; on French, 134-137; on German, 192-194. *See also* International
Compagnonnages, 78-79, 80
Confédération Générale du Travail, formation of, 93-95; policy of, 101-105; union with Federation of Bourses, 98-101; membership, 76, 130, 133; and the War, 120-125; post-War collaboration of, 124-129; the C. G. T. U. secedes from, 135; mentioned, 2, 75, 102. *See also* Syndicalism
Confédération Générale du Travail Unitaire, 135-138
Congress of Industrial Organizations, compared to British New Unionism, 51-52; mentioned, 6
Conservative labor movements, characterized, 2-3, 5
Coöperation, French, 81, 82, 86; German, 148-149, 155-157
Coulson, Edward, 39

De Montgomery, B. G., quoted, 61
Dockers' Strike, 47-50
Duncker, Franz, 151 n

Eisenach, Congress of, 163; mentioned, 164, 165, 166
Engels, Friedrich, 153

Fabians, characterized, 46-47; and the Independent Labor Party, 54-55; compared to the Independent Socialists, 89; and Eduard Bernstein, 182
Federation, National, of Syndicats, 91-93
Federation of Bourses, 97-98; union with C. G. T., 99

Federation of Socialist Workingmen of France, 85
Federations, British trade union, 10-11
Fourier, Charles, 81
Free unions, importance of, 148; and Lassalle, 149; and the Social Democratic Party, 152, 191; and the Christian unions, 187-188; membership, 171, 179, 190, 191; mentioned, 152, 186, 189
French Labor Party, 88, 92, 97. *See also Parti Ouvrier Français*

General Council (of British Trades Union Congress), 14; leadership in miners' dispute, 69-71
General strike, as a weapon of the Grand National Consolidated, 28-29; of Chartism, 31; of syndicalism, 94, 113-116, 129; of the C. G. T. U., 137; Sorel's conception of, 115; Guesdist opposition to, 92-93, 114; of 1926 in Britain, 68-72; of French railroads, 132-133; controversy over in German unions, 175, 178-179
Gompers, Samuel, 2
Gotha, formation of Social Democratic Party at, 166
Grand National Consolidated Trades Union, 27-30, 37
Griffuelhes, Victor, 104
Guesde, Jules, 86, 87, 88
Guesdists, and the National Federation of Syndicats, 92, 97; and the general strike, 114; Marxian orthodoxy of, 88; mentioned, 89
Guilds, craftsmens', related to the British trade union, 15-16; German, 149

Halberstadt, first General Trade Union Congress at, 170, 173-174
Hardie, Keir, 55
Hatzfeldt, Countess, 153, 164
Hirsch, Max, 150-151

INDEX

Hirsch-Duncker unions, 151-152; membership, 171, 191; mentioned, 2, 148, 158, 163, 186
Hitler, Adolph, 139
Hodges, Frank, 68
Hornby versus Close decision, 40

Independent Labor Party (British), 53-55; secedes from Labor Party, 63
Independent Socialist Party, German, 191, 192; French, 89
Industrial revolution, effect of on British labor, 16-17; on German, 142-144
International, First Socialist, influence on French labor, 83, 86, 161; and the general strike, 113; Second Socialist and May Day, 177; Third or Communist, 129-130; and the C. G. T. U., 134-138; and the general strike, 178; Amsterdam, 134, 178, 179

Jaurès, Jean, 89, 122
Joad, C. E. M., on syndicalism, 106
Jouhaux, Léon, on the Marseilles Congress, 85; on social revolution, 128; and the C. G. T. shift to the right, 122, 124, 129, 138; mentioned, 130, 133
"Junta," 39, 41

Kirkup, Thomas, quoted, 145, 161

Labor Front (in Germany), 140
Labor movement, defined, 1-2
Labor Party (British), formed, 52-56; influenced by the Taff Vale decision, 58; point of view and conduct, 60-64; French, see French Labor Party
Labor Representation Committee, 55
Laissez faire, in Britain, 17-18; and the New Model, 34-35
Lassalle, Ferdinand, 150, 153-158; versus Marx, 158-161; and co-operation, 149; mentioned, 145, 151, 164

Legien, Karl, 179
Levine, Louis, on syndicalism and socialist factions, 90; on the C. G. T., 93
"Lib-Labism," 53, 61
Liebknecht, William, 162-163; on the imminence of social revolution, 172
Localists, 169-170
Louis, Paul, on the C. G. T., 106; on syndicalism, 108

MacDonald, J. Ramsay, 55, 56, 63-64
Malthus, Thomas, 21-22
Mann, Tom, quoted, 43-44; mentioned, 45, 48, 49
Mannheim Agreement, 179-180, 183, 184
Marx, Karl, on capitalistic decline, 3-5; versus Lassalle, 158-161; and the general strike, 113-114; mentioned, 15, 53, 153, 153 n, 162, 181, 190
Marxism, and British labor, 45; and French, 87, 88; and German, 161-164; mentioned, 92, 181. *See also* Marx; Revisionism
May Day, observance of discontinued by C. G. T., 124; of 1919 in Paris, 131; first German, 173; and socialist-trade union dissension in Germany, 175, 177
Mill, J. S., on the wages fund theory, 23
Millerand, A., 89, 112
Montgomery, B. G. De, quoted, 61
Mutualités, 78, 79-80

Napoleon I, penal code of, 77
Napoleon III, 81
National Federation of Syndicats, 91-93, 98
National Socialism, 139-141
New Model, 33-36; unions typical of, 37-38; decline of, 43; and the New Unionism, 44-45, 49; mentioned, 2, 47, 50, 52

New Unionism, British, beginnings of, 43-45; and socialism, 44-47; and the Dockers' Strike, 48-52; mentioned, 6, 52; in America, 50-52

O'Connor, Fergus, 38
Odger, R., 39
Osborne judgment, 59-60
Owen, Robert, program of, 28; mentioned, 27, 38, 46

Parliamentary Committee (British), 13, 53
Parti Ouvrier Français, 88, 97
Parti Socialiste Unifié, 103
Pelloutier, Fernand, 97
Perlman, Selig, quoted 9, 180
Place, Francis, 25, 27
Pouget, Émile, 114
Proudhon, J. P., 81, 87, 109

Reformism, 125-129
Reform Bill (British of 1832), and Owen's program, 28; and Chartism, 30; mentioned, 52
Republic (German), status of trade unionism within, 141, 189-191; mentioned, 194
Revisionism (in Germany), 180-185
Revolution, French, and British labor, 24-25; and French labor, 77, 110; of 1848, and French labor, 80, 81, 82, 110; of 1848, and German labor, 168; of 1848, mentioned, 81; Russian, and British labor, 73; and French labor, 119, 120, 127-128
Revolutionary Socialist Party (French), 88
Ricardo, David, theory of on wages, 156, 159 n
Rodbertus, Karl, 153
Royal Commission (British), and the miners' strike, 67; and the general strike of 1926, 69

Sabotage, 116-117
Saint-Simon, Comte Henri de, 81
Samuel Memorandum, 71
Say, J. B., 81
Schulze, Herman, and coöperation, 148-149; versus Lassalle, 155-157; mentioned, 158, 159
Schulze-Delitzsch. See Schulze
Schweitzer, von, J. V., 164
"Sheffield Outrage," 40
Smith, Adam, 18, 21
Snowden, Philip, 63-64
Social Democratic Federation (British), 54, 56
Social Democratic Party (German), and the Free unions, 152, 163-164, 192; formation of, 157-163, 166; outlawed, 166-168; triumph of, 171-172; and the Mannheim Agreement, 174-180; Revisionism, 180-185; split in, 191; mentioned, 189
Socialism, and syndicalism, 107-108; and the New Unionism, 44-46
Sociétés de résistance, 78, 80, 82
Sorel, Georges, theory of the general strike, 115
Syndicalism, defined, 75; revolutionary nature of, 98, 105-106; and anarchism, 106-107, 109-110; and Marxian socialism, 107-108; methods of, 113-119; antimilitarism of, 118-119, 121; antipolitical attitude of, 104, 133, 134-135; reformist, 125-129. See also Confédération Générale du Travail

Taff Vale decision, 56-58, 59
Thomas, J. H., 63-64
Tillet, Ben, 45, 48, 49
Trades councils (British), 11
Trades' unions (American), compared to the bourses du travail, 96

Trades Union Congress (British), 11-14; general council of, 14, 69-71
Trade unions (British), characterized, 8-10
Triple Alliance, 67-68

Universal Workingmen's Association (German), 157, 162, 163

Value, Marxian theory of, 4
Villeneuve-Saint-Georges, 111
Viviani, René, 89, 112

Wages, rise of in Britain in the 1850's, 32, 36; and post-War adjustments in Britain, 66-68; iron law of, 156-157, 159-160; the wages fund doctrine, 22-23, 27
Waldeck-Rousseau, René, 90
Walras, M., 81
Webb, Sidney and Beatrice, quoted, 39, 41
Workers' Educational Association (German), 161
Works councils, 193-194
Works Councils Act of 1920, 193
World War I, and British labor, 64-68; and French, 119-129; and German, 184-185, 188-191

Yellow unions, 147 n

Zollverein, 143, 144

www.ingramcontent.com/pod-product-compliance
Lightning Source LLC
Chambersburg PA
CBHW021124300426
44113CB00006B/285